LEIBNIZ: A GUIDE FOR THE PERPLEXED

LEIBNIZ: A GUIDE FOR THE PERPLEXED

FRANKLIN PERKINS

continuum

CONTINUUM
Continuum International Publishing Group
The Tower Building   80 Maiden Lane
11 York Road   Suite 704
London SE1 7NX   New York
                           NY 10038

www.continuumbooks.com

British Library Cataloguing-in-Publication Data
A catalogue record for this book is available from the British Library.

ISBN: HB: 0-8264-8920-6
9780826489203
PB: 0-8264-8921-4
9780826489210

Library of Congress Cataloging-in-Publication Data
A catalog record for this book is available from the Library of Congress.

Typeset by Acorn Bookwork Ltd, Salisbury, Wiltshire
Printed and bound in Great Britain by
Athenaeum Press Ltd, Gateshead, Tyne & Wear

CONTENTS

ACKNOWLEDGEMENTS

This book owes a great debt to Emily Grosholz, who first enabled me to see Leibniz as something more than eccentric and outdated. Her influence shapes my basic approach to Leibniz and many of the specific points I make here. I am also grateful to Amanda Parris, who gave me helpful feedback on the entire manuscript and did much of the tedious work involved in preparing it. I would also like to thank Robin Wang, who read through the manuscript and gave me many helpful comments. Much of my knowledge of Leibniz derives from a research grant from the Deutscher An Akademischer Austauschdienst (DAAD) which allowed me to spend a year at the Leibniz Archive. I am grateful to Herbert Breger and Rita Widmaier for their considerable help there. I am fortunate to be in a department enthusiastic about both researching and teaching the history of philosophy. This manuscript shows the influence of many conversations both with my colleagues and students. Finally, I would like to thank the editors at Continuum Press, particularly Nick Fawcett for his careful copy-editing

My greatest debt is to my parents, particularly for always encouraging me to pursue what I loved, in spite of what appeared to be a dubious economic future. I would not be writing this book but for scholarships from Vanderbilt University, the Richardson Foundation, and the Citizen's Scholarship Foundation, all of which made it possible for me to attend college in the first place. I will always be grateful for that support.

Quotations from Roger Ariew and Daniel Garber (ed. and trans.), *Philosophical Essays*, 1989, reprinted by permission of Hackett Publishing Company, Inc. All rights reserved.

ACKNOWLEDGEMENTS

Quotations from Peter Remnant and Jonathan Bennett (trans.), *New Essays on the Human Understanding*, 1981, reprinted by permission of Cambridge University Press. All rights reserved.

Quotations from R.S. Woolhouse and R. Francks (ed. and trans.), *Philosophical Texts*, 1998, reprinted by permission of Oxford University Press. All rights reserved.

ABBREVIATIONS

A: *Sämtliche Schriften und Briefe*, ed. Deutsche Akademie der Wissenschaften (Darmstadt/Leipzig/Berlin: Akademie Verlag, 1923–). Cited by series, volume, and page number.

AG: *Philosophical Essays*, ed. and trans. Roger Ariew and Daniel Garber (Indianapolis: Hackett, 1989). Cited by page number.

DM: *Discourse on Metaphysics*. Cited by section number. (See AG for bibliographical details.)

M: *Monadology*. Cited by section number. (See AG for bibliographical details.)

NE: *New Essays on the Human Understanding*, trans. Peter Remnant and Jonathan Bennett (Cambridge: Cambridge University Press, 1981). Cited by page number.

PNG: *Principles of Nature and Grace, Based on Reason*. Cited by section number.

T: *Theodicy: Essays on the Goodness of God, the Freedom of Man, and the Origin of Evil*, trans. E. M. Huggard (Chicago: Open Court, 1985). Cited by page number.

WF: *Philosophical Texts*, trans. and ed. R. S. Woolhouse and R. Francks (Oxford: Oxford University Press, 1998). Cited by page number.

CHAPTER I

READING LEIBNIZ

I. CONTEXT OF LEIBNIZ'S PHILOSOPHY

Substances do not interact. Every substance is eternal. Bodies are phenomena, not independently real. Choices are determined but free. This is the best possible world. I first encountered Leibniz in an introduction to Modern Philosophy and the image of him as a philosopher so enthralled with his reasoning as to deny the reality in front of him stuck with me for a long time. It wasn't that his arguments were bad, but that their conclusions seemed obviously false. Wouldn't a swift kick in the shin suffice to prove that substances do interact, that bodies are real, and perhaps even that this is not the best possible world? This image of Leibniz as naïve and detached from reality was cemented by Voltaire's satirical character Dr Pangloss, who insists over and over again – in the face of the worst suffering and injustice – that this is the best possible world.[1] There is some irony in this image of Leibniz, as Leibniz was the far opposite of an 'ivory tower' philosopher. He consistently pursued positions that would increase his political influence over positions that would increase his leisure for study and reflection. Leibniz claimed the progress of knowledge as his main goal, but he approached this goal from two sides, on one side through his own research and writing while on the other side promoting institutions that would better support, disseminate, and apply knowledge. Today, Leibniz is best known or at least most widely read for his philosophical writings, but philosophy represents only a small part of his life's work. Although this book will focus on explaining Leibniz's philosophy, that philosophy must be approached from within the broader context of his life and time.

Gottfried Wilhelm Leibniz was born in Leipzig, Germany, on 1 July 1646.[2] His father was a professor of moral philosophy at the University of Leipzig, but died when Leibniz was six years old. His mother was the daughter of a prominent lawyer and died when Leibniz was 17. Leibniz entered school at an early age, but he largely taught himself by reading in his father's extensive library – he was fluent in Latin by age 12. In a passage explaining some of the characteristics of his thought, Leibniz gives this account of his own training:

> Two things marvelously benefited me in this (things otherwise problematic, however, and often harmful to many): first, that I was nearly self-taught and, second, that I sought out what was new in each and every branch of knowledge, as soon as I came into contact with it, even though I often had not yet sufficiently grasped things commonly known. But these two things gave me this advantage; the first prevented me from filling my mind with trifles, things that ought to be forgotten, things that are accepted on the authority of teachers rather than because of arguments, and the second prevented me from resting before I probed all the way to the depths of each subject and arrived at its very principles, from which everything I extracted could be discovered by my own efforts. (AG 6)

On finishing university studies in philosophy and law, Leibniz was offered a teaching position at the University of Altdorf, but he declined it, instead taking a political position under the Elector of Mainz, Johann Philipp von Schönborn. At age 24 he was appointed to the High Court of Appeal, helped revise the legal code, and assisted in various political schemes, such as drafting a detailed plan to convince Louis XIV to invade Egypt instead of Holland. After the death of his main patron in Mainz and a few years living in Paris, he took a position in 1676 as Counsellor and then Privy Counsellor to the Duke of Hannover, Johann Friedrich. He remained in this position, serving three different rulers, until his death on 14 November 1716. He never married or had children and in spite of the massive amount that he wrote, little is known of his personal life.

Leibniz is often referred to as a 'universal genius'. The breadth of his interests and accomplishments is difficult to comprehend.

He lived near the end of a time when an intelligent, well-connected person could know the current developments in almost all areas of European knowledge, but even in that context Leibniz was exceptional for his ability to contribute to so many fields. In his own time, Leibniz was probably most significant as a mathematician. Among his contributions to that field was his invention of calculus around the same time as Isaac Newton. He made significant contributions to physics, particularly through his analysis of force, and wrote essays on related fields such as optics and astronomy. In philosophy, much of his focus was on what we might call 'philosophical theology'; his *Theodicy* remains one of the greatest attempts to reconcile the goodness of God with the existence of a world that does not seem so good. He made important contributions to the development of logic and the theory of signs, which were part of his overall focus on questions of methodology. Leibniz also examined issues that might now fall under psychology – his 'minute perceptions' foreshadow ideas about the subconscious that have become widely accepted. Beside these theoretical interests, Leibniz was concerned with technology and what we might call 'applied science'. He first came to serious attention in intellectual circles because of an adding machine he invented. He spent considerable time designing and constructing a new system for pumping water from mines using windmills. All of this work was done along with his duties managing the library and archives in Hannover and serving as a public policy advisor not only to the court in Hannover but to anyone who would listen, including Emperor Karl IV, who appointed him Imperial Privy Counsellor, and Czar Peter the Great, who appointed him Privy Counsellor of Justice. In his role as advisor, Leibniz drafted proposals on almost every topic, from economics, to controlling the plague, to proper treatment of soldiers. One result of his policy efforts was the founding of the Berlin Society of Sciences in 1700, of which he was the first president. He was also often involved in complex, sometimes secret, political negotiations, the most significant of which was the passing of the English throne to Leibniz's patron, Elector Georg Ludwig, who subsequently became King George I of England. Although he is little known for it, Leibniz spent much of his life researching and writing an extensive history of the House of Brunswick-Luneburg, by whom he was employed. Although never completed, he published a few volumes of this history, along with two collections of archival documents, mostly concerning international law and relations.

What was the place of philosophy in this long list of activities? Although Leibniz conducted some experiments and collected some data, this was not his strength or his focus. His scientific contributions came more from thinking through problems carefully and coherently rather than from discovering new evidence through his own experiments. Leibniz was a systematic thinker with an incredible ability to draw together a wide range of ideas. He was fundamentally concerned with coherence and had little patience for scientific explanations that described experience accurately but ultimately made no sense. For example, he was dissatisfied with Newton's theory of gravity not because it failed to provide an accurate account of experience – Leibniz recognized that it did – but because it did not make sense in relation to then current ideas of causality. In an essay entitled 'Against Barbaric Physics', directed primarily at Newton, Leibniz writes, 'It is permissible to recognize magnetic, elastic, and other sorts of forces, but only insofar as we understand that they are not primitive or incapable of being explained, but arise from motions and shapes' (AG 313). For Leibniz and his contemporaries, it was impossible for one thing to act on another thing without some physical contact between them. If there could be no 'action at a distance', how could one body attract another body across space? In that context, gravitational forces made about as much sense as telekinesis or extra-sensory perception do now. For Leibniz, gravity remained insufficient as an explanation so long as there was no way to understand the possibility of attraction at a distance. In this approach to science, the role of Leibniz's philosophy was largely to render his more empirical, practical concerns coherent. For example, Leibniz believed that scientific explanation depended on what he calls the principle of sufficient reason: that for any event there must be reasons why it happens this way rather than another. Experimental method relies on this principle: experiments conducted under the same conditions should get the same results, because a difference in effects would require a difference in causes. For Leibniz, it would not be acceptable to assume this principle in practice if it proved to be incoherent in theory. Much of Leibniz's philosophy is dedicated to showing how the principle of sufficient reason can be maintained in relation to God and God's creation of the world. Similarly, Leibniz's theory of substance is meant to render accounts of the physical world in terms of aggregation coherent by placing substances – the true unities that are the basic constituents of reality – outside the material world. Leibniz's most counter-intuitive claims generally serve to reconcile the demands of reason with more pragmatic accounts of experience. In other words, Leibniz's philosophy often begins with the question – given that our experience is this particular way, what must be true in order for that to be possible and intelligible? This commitment to accurate accounts of experience and to theoretical coherence is perhaps the defining characteristic of Leibniz's philosophy.

A thorough discussion of Leibniz's broader context would exceed the limits of this book, but three factors must be briefly considered. The first is war. Leibniz was born near the end of the Thirty Years War (1618–48), which devastated much of central Europe, particularly Germany. Throughout his lifetime, Europe was in a continual state of political struggle and almost continual state of open war. France itself was at war for most of Leibniz's life, with major conflicts lasting from 1672–8, 1688–97, and 1701–14. In addition, the 'Great Northern War' was fought around the Baltic from 1700–21, and the 'Great Turkish War' lasted from 1683–99. Leibniz saw these wars as the greatest obstacle to the common good and even to the progress of science and knowledge, which required stability and free exchange of ideas. These wars cannot be separated from the second important historical factor, which is the fragmentation of European Christianity. The Protestant Reformation had begun in the early sixteenth century and by the time of Leibniz there were numerous conflicting Christian factions, often implicated in politics. Because religious differences often aligned with political divisions, Leibniz believed that reconciling Christian factions was a crucial part of bringing peace to Europe. Leibniz pursued this goal through political manoeuvring, several times engaging in detailed negotiations trying to establish a framework for reconciliation.[3] These concerns shape his philosophy in several ways. For example, his focus on explaining and harmonizing different perspectives cannot be separated from his concern for harmonizing conflicts between religious factions. His attempt to establish a rational, natural theology was part of an attempt to promote a core of Christianity that everyone could agree upon.

The most important factor influencing Leibniz's philosophical thought is the rapid growth of science in the seventeenth century. These scientific developments had a number of consequences for the philosophies of Leibniz and his contemporaries. Perhaps the most important was a deep faith in human knowledge. Leibniz not only believed that science would continue to develop, but that this progress would extend to all areas of human thought, resulting in a substantial improvement in the quality of human life. He thought that the greatest way to improve the human condition was to promote the growth of knowledge, and much of his public activities were dedicated to this goal. A second consequence was a concern for methodology. The rapid growth of science was generally not attributed to the greater genius of modern thinkers but rather to the discovery of proper scientific method. Like his contemporaries, Leibniz was concerned that philosophy lagged behind the sciences, and he blamed this condition on philosophy's lack of suitable method. One of his main goals was to bring the methods of mathematics to bear on philosophy: 'Who could doubt that reasoning will finally be correct, when it is everywhere as clear and certain as arithmetic has been up until now' (AG 8). A third consequence was an increased freedom in questioning assumptions. This freedom most obviously appears as a greater freedom from Church doctrines, but it also emerged as a freedom from the assumptions of common sense. After all, what could conflict more with common sense than the claim that the earth moves around the sun? Does it really feel like you are now moving at a hundred thousand kilometres an hour? The development of science showed that the structure of the universe might be quite different from our everyday experience. This willingness to accept ultimate explanations that conflict with common sense is partly responsible for the creativity that characterizes early modern metaphysics.

In his commitment to science, Leibniz clearly fits his times, but within his own context, he is relatively critical of 'modern' thought and science. He scolds his contemporaries, particularly René Descartes, for being too drawn to fame and innovation. He remarks often that ancient and medieval philosophers cannot be easily dismissed, and he himself rehabilitates a number of unmodern ideas, particularly through his concept of substance. The centre of his criticism of modern thought is his fear that some modern thinkers undermine the key truths of 'natural theology'. 'Natural theology' refers to those truths of religion that can be discovered by reason alone, without reliance on faith or divine revelation. The two key claims of natural theology were the existence of a good God and a just afterlife. Leibniz presents his thought as one of harmony and moderation – reconciling science and religion, ancient and modern, nature and grace. Leibniz never sees this reconciliation, though, as a compromise or weakening of science. Rather, he believes that scientific principles require natural theology. He quotes with approval a saying of Francis Bacon, 'that a little philosophy inclineth us away from God, but that depth in philosophy bringeth men's minds about to him' (T 306). Leibniz did not believe in a conflict between science and theology, only a conflict between *bad* science and theology.

II. DIFFICULTIES OF READING LEIBNIZ

The greatest difficulty in understanding Leibniz's philosophy is grasping the relationship between his more abstract and counter-intuitive metaphysical claims and his more pragmatic social and scientific concerns. Seeing the plausibility and relevance of his philosophy today requires bridging this gap. The very nature of Leibniz's writings, however, creates more fundamental problems for understanding his thought. Leibniz wrote an immense amount. The complete works of Leibniz is projected to have over 40 volumes. These writings match his broad interests, covering an immense variety of topics, only a small part of which is directly philosophical. Many of these writings are short, with a large part consisting of letters. In spite of this immense amount of writing, Leibniz never wrote a full, systematic explanation of his philosophy, so the study of Leibniz's philosophy must draw together many different sources. The most valuable are the few systematic summaries of his philosophy, particularly the *Monadology* and the *Principles of Nature and Grace, Based on Reason*. Both were written near the end of his life and represent his philosophy in its most mature form. These works, though, are more like outlines than full arguments or explanations. They must be supplemented with other materials, bringing together Leibniz's correspondence, his essays on specific topics, and his two books, the *New Essays on the Human Understanding* and the *Theodicy*. The last two works often contain Leibniz's fullest explanations, but neither presents his philosophy completely or systematically.

Aside from the difficulties in finding a path through the labyrinth of Leibniz's writings, several characteristics of his philosophical style make interpreting him difficult. These characteristics can be broadly grouped under four ideas – interconnection, harmony of perspectives, dialogue, and expression. All four are central both to Leibniz's philosophy and his way of expressing that philosophy. We can begin with interconnection. In his *Meditations on First Philosophy* Descartes asks for an 'Archimedian point', an undeniable foundation on which he could base the rest of his philosophy: 'Archimedes used to demand just one firm and immovable point in order to shift the entire earth; so I too can hope for great things if I manage to find just one thing, however slight, that is certain and unshakeable.'[4] The certainty of our own existence provided that point, from which Descartes could prove that God exists and is good, and from there the rest of his philosophy. We can call this method 'foundational'. Such a method was often modelled on geometrical proof and was sometimes compared to a chain – each link follows in a line, with each depending entirely on the strength of the link before it. Although Leibniz sometimes praises this method, his philosophy does not rely so much on one foundation but rather on the interdependence of many different principles. Each of those principles gains strength from the others, with the ultimate strength of his philosophy depending on its ability to give an efficient and coherent account of experience. A single principle thus frequently plays key roles in multiple areas and arguments. This interconnection of principles and concepts fits Leibniz's claim that everything in the world is connected, but it makes it difficult to understand any part of Leibniz's philosophy in isolation from the whole, which makes an initial approach extremely difficult – each part can only be understood in relation to the whole, but we must begin somewhere, with some particular part. Furthermore, this interconnection of principles often extends to Leibniz's other interests; it is not unusual to find key philosophical discussions in the midst of an essay on motion, to find discussions of physics or biology in the midst of a philosophical essay, or to find Leibniz illustrating a philosophical point with a complex mathematical problem. Chapter 1 begins with two of Leibniz's key epistemological principles and then moves to his account of God as the metaphysical foundation for the world, but both the meaning and strength of these positions will only become fully clear as the reader continues toward an understanding of Leibniz's philosophy as a whole.

The second characteristic of Leibniz's philosophy is a desire to harmonize different perspectives. The fundamental metaphor Leibniz uses to explain the relationships among minds is different points of view on the same city: 'Indeed, *all individual created substances are different expressions of the same universe* and different expressions of the same universal cause, namely God. But the expressions vary in perfection, just as different representations or drawings of the same town from different points of view do' (AG 33). Leibniz's concern for 'point of view' deeply shapes his own approach to philosophy. On a practical level, this awareness of both the truth and limits of any particular point of view drives an imperative to increase exchange and interaction between diverse perspectives. That concern attains its most striking expression in Leibniz's promotion of cultural exchange with China, but also appears in his promotion of learned societies, journals, and even in his own reliance on correspondence. In his philosophy, this focus on perspective appears in his attempt to reconcile and harmonize different points of view. The character 'Theophilus' describes Leibniz's own philosophy in the *New Essays*: 'This system appears to unite Plato with Democritus, Aristotle with Descartes, the Scholastics with the moderns, theology and morality with reason. Apparently it takes the best from all systems and then advances further than anyone has yet done' (NE 71). This tendency toward harmonizing different points of view can be misleading. For the sake of harmony, Leibniz sometimes obscures the extent to which he modifies the thought of others in order to incorporate them into his own philosophy. As a result, one must be careful to distinguish the meaning that Leibniz gives to the terms and positions he borrows from other philosophers.

This concern for point of view naturally leads Leibniz to emphasize dialogue. Leibniz was a philosopher of dialogue, not just because he wrote some dialogues but because most of what he wrote was written in response to or for particular people. Leibniz carried on an immense correspondence, with people ranging from intellectual giants like Antoine Arnauld and Christopher Huygens to political giants like Peter the Great and to people as far away as the Jesuit missionaries living in China. The systematic outlines of his philosophy that we most rely on were all written for specific people – the *Discourse on Metaphysics* for Antoine Arnauld and the *Monadology* for Nicholas Remond. Even Leibniz's works intended for a general audience were mostly written as responses to particular people. For example, Leibniz's *New Essays on the Human Understanding* was written in response to John Locke's *Essays on the Human Understanding*. Leibniz writes it as a dialogue, in which Philalethes represents the views of Locke and Theophilus represents Leibniz. The book follows the same order as Locke's book and the words of Philalethes are almost all quotations from Locke, so it really is more a commentary than an independent work. While the *Theodicy* was not written as a dialogue, it responds point by point to claims made by Pierre Bayle, with appendices responding to other thinkers, like Thomas Hobbes. Leibniz's tendency to write in particular dialogues leads to the most significant problems for interpreting his writing. As with most philosophers, Leibniz is concerned with promoting his own philosophy but he did so not primarily through thorough explanations meant to convince any reader but rather by persuading particular people in particular contexts. Consequently, he often presents his ideas in the way that will most likely persuade his particular audience. For example in the *Discourse on Metaphysics*, Leibniz quotes scripture and ends with a passage praising Jesus, but the essay was intended for Antoine Arnauld, a leading Catholic theologian and philosopher. Leibniz spends considerable energy trying to reconcile his philosophy with Catholic sacraments like transubstantiation, but it is unlikely that he himself took those sacraments seriously.[5] In general, Leibniz appears more Catholic when writing to Catholics and more Protestant when writing to Protestants, more cosmopolitan when writing to foreigners and more patriotic when writing to Germans. This way of writing may reflect a manipulative and political side of Leibniz's personality, but it also expresses a genuine concern for building common ground by making his philosophy intelligible and applicable in different contexts. In any case, this tendency means that Leibniz sometimes describes his philosophy in ways that are quite misleading; one must read him carefully, attending to writings from a variety of contexts and to the overall coherence of his thought.

The fourth characteristic of Leibniz's philosophy employs one of his key philosophical concepts, *expression*. Leibniz explains expression as that which

> is said to express a thing in which there are relations which correspond to the relations of the thing expressed. But there are various kinds of expression; for example, the model of a machine expresses the machine itself, a projective delineation on a plane expresses a solid, speech expresses thoughts and truths, characters express numbers, and an algebraic equation expresses a circle or some other figure. What is common to all these expressions is that we can pass from a consideration of the relations in the expression to a knowledge of the corresponding properties of the thing expressed.[6]

Leibniz invokes expression to explain many particular relationships, but on a general level expression serves to coordinate things that have no intrinsic similarity. For example, a city map is small, flat, light, foldable, and so on, all completely different from a city. What is the relationship between the map and the city? Leibniz calls the relationship one of expression, which means that the relationships between items on the map correspond to the relationships between things in the city itself. That is, the two express the same set of relationships, which is why one can be used to navigate the other in spite of their radical differences. In terms of writing, expression can be taken as a theory of translation, explaining how one can express the same chain of ideas in radically different languages or symbols. Leibniz utilizes this idea of expression to justify speaking of the same thing in very different ways. For example, speaking with metaphysical rigour, substances do not interact and thus lack direct causal relations, yet Leibniz does not hesitate to discuss phenomena in terms of interaction and causality. Both ways of speaking are valid because causal terms express the real (but non-causal) relationships between substances. Leibniz's account of causality will be discussed in chapter 3, but the important point is that Leibniz is quite willing to talk about things on different levels. He gives this a theoretical justification in an essay on reconciling Copernicanism with the language of the Bible, saying,

And on this matter we must reply that one should choose the more intelligible hypothesis, and that the truth of a hypothesis is nothing but its intelligibility. Now, from a different point of view, not with respect to people and their opinions, but with respect to the very things we need to deal with, one hypothesis might be more intelligible than another and more appropriate for a given purpose. And so, from different points of view, the one might be true and the other false. Thus, for a hypothesis to be true is just for it to be properly used. (AG 91)

A good hypothesis explains things within a certain context, so that different contexts require different ways of talking and the same description might be true in one context and false in another. The problem with this approach is that Leibniz will often say things in one context that he would consider false in another. He occasionally warns us that he is speaking this way – he says he will speak in the same way that Copernicans continue to speak of the rising sun (NE 74) – but often he does not warn us. Again, the best solution is to read widely and to attend to the overall coherence of his philosophy.

III. USING THIS BOOK

One can read Leibniz, or the history of philosophy, for many reasons: to understand the history of European thought, to find old but neglected ideas that might be useful now, or to find good philosophical arguments. Perhaps the fundamental reason to read the history of philosophy, though, is to engage the world from a perspective different from our own. Reading Leibniz gives us a chance to see how one of the greatest philosophical minds saw the world, starting from assumptions, experiences, and concerns quite different from our own. Even if we ultimately reject his assumptions and even his conclusions, the difference in perspective cannot help but illuminate the limits of our own context and the rich ways in which human experience can be theorized. To see the world from the point of view of Leibniz is an unattainable goal – we cannot so fully escape our own context. The hope is to approach this ideal, but even that is quite difficult. We must struggle to see Leibniz's claims not just in our context but also in his. This struggle takes patience and a certain slowness to pass judgement, something that philosophers sometimes find particularly difficult. I often warn my students that if a great philosopher says something stupid or obviously false, you have not understood what they are saying. It is not that understanding a philosopher requires seeing that they are right, but it requires seeing what they say as a plausible meeting between their historical context and our common human experience.

The best way to reach this kind of understanding of a philosopher is to read what they have written. When that proves difficult, as it inevitably does, the best response is to read more of what they have written and then to read it again and again and again. Only after this kind of struggle with the original texts is it advisable to start reading what other philosophers have written about them. At the same time, one cannot even begin to read a philosopher without some context and guidance. This is particularly true for Leibniz, whose claims often seem so strange and whose voluminous writings are so difficult to navigate. The goal of this book is to enable readers to read Leibniz for themselves. It attempts as much as possible to present Leibniz in his own terms and even in his own words, avoiding inserting contemporary philosophical terms and debates into his context. It includes little evaluation or criticism of his philosophy and little explicit discussion of current debates or applications of his philosophy or its influence on later philosophers. While all of these are useful, they should follow from rather than precede a basic understanding of Leibniz's philosophy. Helping readers reach that basic understanding is the goal of this book.

More specifically, this book tries to do three things. First, it brings together discussions scattered throughout Leibniz's vast corpus so as to present his main ideas as fully as possible. Second, it tries to reveal the coherence of his philosophy by bringing out the complex web of connections between his main claims. There are tensions within Leibniz's philosophy and several issues on which his thought changed and evolved over time. This book includes some discussion of these tensions but not the evolution of Leibniz's thinking, focusing only on explaining Leibniz's 'mature' thought, relying primarily on the *Monadology*, *Principles of Nature and Grace, Based on Reason*, the *New Essays on the Human Understanding*, and the *Theodicy*. Third, I have tried to present Leibniz's views as plausible, insightful accounts of human experience. This has required on one side giving some account of the context in which he writes while on the other side bridging between that context and our own experience. In doing so, my hope is that this book will not only allow readers to better understand Leibniz but will also allow them to see how his insights and analyses still shed light on our experience.

CHAPTER 2

GOD AND THE BEST POSSIBLE WORLD

I. TWO PRINCIPLES OF KNOWLEDGE

Although Leibniz's philosophy has no single foundation, Leibniz names two principles as essential for all human knowledge, even saying that these two principles are implied in the very definitions of truth and falsity (T 419). The first is the *principle of contradiction*, sometimes called the principle of identity or of non-contradiction. He writes in a letter to Samuel Clarke:

> The great foundation of mathematics is the principle of contradiction or identity, that is, that a proposition cannot be true and false at the same time, and that therefore A is A and cannot be not A. This single principle is sufficient to demonstrate every part of arithmetic and geometry, that is, all mathematical principles. (AG 321)

The principle of contradiction states that 'A' and 'not-A' cannot both be true, or that nothing can be both true and false at the same time and in the same way. Leibniz calls the principle of contradiction a 'primitive truth of reason'. We know it by intuition – if we think about it clearly, we simply know that it is true. As a primitive truth, it cannot be proven. In fact, this principle is implicit in the very concept of proof; any proof for it would have to already assume it. The principle is thus justified both by an appeal to intuition but also by the fact that we do accept the validity of logic and mathematics. If we accept these, then we must accept the principle of contradiction. In other words, to reason is just to apply this principle: denying it amounts to denying the possibility of any reasoning. More simply, if one friend tells you that he was at home watching television last night and another friend tells you she saw him out dancing last night, you assume that one of those two friends is mistaken or lying. Their statements contradict and so cannot both be true. We perform this kind of reasoning all the time, although without any awareness of something called the 'principle of contradiction'.

The second fundamental principle is that of sufficient reason. In the *Monadology*, Leibniz explains that the *principle of sufficient reason* is that 'by virtue of which we consider that we can find no true or existent fact, no true assertion, without there being a sufficient reason why it is thus and not otherwise, although most of the time these reasons cannot be known to us' (M 32; AG 217). For any thing or event, there must be reasons sufficient to explain why this thing exists rather than some other thing, or why this event occurred rather than some other event. More simply, every effect must have a cause. As with the principle of contradiction, Leibniz considers this principle to be a primary truth that is justified primarily by the fact that we actually do rely on it. To deny the principle of sufficient reason would be to deny most of human knowledge, in particular, any knowledge of actually existing things. We rely on the principle of sufficient reason whenever we ask why, and expect that, at least in principle, there should be an answer. We see this reliance most clearly in experimental method. We assume that an experiment can be repeated and that if the same experiment yields different results, there must have been some difference in the experiments. If we did not rely on the principle of sufficient reason, we would have to admit that the identical experiment could yield different results for no reason at all. The principle also operates on a more mundane level. Whenever we meet an unexpected event, we make sense of it by searching for its causes. Imagine you are home alone and hear a voice telling you to take the *Monadology* off the bookshelf and read it. You would first check the door and search the apartment to see if someone was there. If not, you might look for a hidden speaker some place. If you still found nothing, you would move on to less plausible explanations – perhaps it was a neighbour speaking loudly, or the voice of a ghost or angel, or perhaps you were hallucinating. We would be pushed to these speculations because we would never doubt that the voice must have some cause. That it was produced by a ghost is unlikely, but that it happened with no cause at all is impossible. This kind of reasoning, which we use all the time in our everyday lives, reveals our deep reliance on the principle of sufficient reason. The intuitive ground of this principle is more apparent if we consider it as a version of the principle that every effect must have a cause, which itself applies the principle that something cannot come from nothing. The characteristics of a thing are real and thus could not come from nothing; they must have come from some other thing which caused them and provides a reason for their existence. Without such a cause, the characteristics would come from nothing.

Although both principles seem obvious and unremarkable, much of Leibniz's philosophy comes simply from thinking through all of the consequences which follow from them. We can consider an example – what is the sufficient reason for my writing on this particular notebook? We might mention several reasons: I agreed to write this book, I still prefer to write on paper rather than computer; I was in the office and needed a new notebook, there was a stack of them in the cabinet and this one was on top. This answer might be adequate, depending on our purpose in asking the question, but these reasons do not supply a fully *sufficient* explanation. Instead, they raise more questions. We could pursue any of them; for example, why I am writing this book? The reasons would have to include why I studied Leibniz, why I became a philosopher at all, how I went to college, even the circumstances of my birth. These reasons, though, lead to still more questions. In the end, we would have to explain the lives of my parents, the development of the United States, immigration from Northern Europe, the evolution of the human species, and the origins of our solar system. We could find just as many reasons if we turned to the factory which produced the notebook, the invention of paper and its transmission to Europe, the evolution of trees, and so on.

Imagine a persistent child asking 'why?' to every reason we give. If we had infinite knowledge and patience, we would find ourselves eventually describing the whole universe and its history. In other words, the sufficient reason for the existence of any particular thing involves the whole world. For Leibniz, this reflects the fact that all things are interconnected, so that a change in one part of the world causes at least slight changes in everything else. For me to exist as a carpenter rather than as writing a book on Leibniz would require this to be a different world, not only because of the difference in me but because that difference would require differences in the reasons that produced me, which would require differences in the reasons that produced those, and so on. The full understanding of any particular existing thing requires an understanding of the whole universe, so that the complete concept of this one notebook involves the entire universe. Leibniz says, '... [h]e who sees all can read in each thing what happens everywhere, and even what has happened or what will happen, by observing in the present what is remote in time as well as space' (M 61; AG 221). Because the whole universe is implicated in my own existence, God's choice to create me rather than someone else is at the same time a choice to create this whole world, and vice versa. Finally, because the complete concept or the fully sufficient reason for any particular thing involves an infinite world, only God can know any one thing perfectly. We can be sure that for any thing there is a sufficient reason, but we can never fully grasp the details of those reasons.

Even if we are led by the principle of sufficient reason to explain this notebook in terms of its implication in the whole world, we still have not given a reason that is fully sufficient. If the child asking why were especially astute, we could predict her next question – why does this particular world exist? Why is there this particular system of causes? We might reply that God created it, but that leads to further questions: not only why did God create this world but why does God exist in the first place? Before looking at Leibniz's specific reply to these questions, we can see a problem inherent in the principle of sufficient reason. Even if we have infinite knowledge and patience, it seems that at some point we will have to say to the child – that is just the way it is! We seem stuck between either positing some first explanation which cannot itself be explained or an infinite regress of explanations with no ultimate cause or reason. The only way out of this problem is to posit something which explains the existence of other things *and* explains its own existence. Leibniz develops this kind of response through the distinction between necessary and contingent truths, a distinction that follows from his distinction between the principle of contradiction and the principle of sufficient reason.

Necessary truths are those whose opposites are impossible; contingent truths are those whose opposites are possible. That is, to say that a thing's existence is contingent is to say that its existence and non-existence are both possible. My existence as a philosopher is a contingent truth, since my existence as a carpenter or even a dentist is intrinsically possible. While my existence as a philosopher follows with certainty from this order of the world, my existence as something else seems intrinsically possible, even though it would require that the world itself be somewhat different. Things that exist contingently fall within the realm of the principle of sufficient reason precisely because they exist as only one of several possible options. Facing several possibilities, there must be some reason to explain which particular one actually exists, that is, there must be a sufficient reason. But what if only one option is possible? If there are no alternatives, then we do not really need a reason to explain why this particular one happens – anything else would be impossible. Such truths fall within the realm of the principle of contradiction. Their opposite is contradictory and thus impossible, which means that they themselves are necessary. We might take this to mean that necessary truths lack a sufficient reason, but it would be better to say that they provide their own reason. Their very nature eliminates all other possibilities and thus explains their own existence. Thus to maintain the principle of sufficient reason coherently, contingent truths must be traced back to necessary truths. The existence of contingent things needing a sufficient reason must ultimately be explained by something that exists necessarily, something that supplies its own reason and the reason for other things.

We can now return to the question about the sufficient reason for the existence of this particular world. Is the existence of this world necessary or contingent? That is, are other worlds possible? One of Leibniz's central claims is that there are other possible worlds. It certainly seems possible that I could have used a different notebook, even if we admit that this difference would require a slight adjustment of the entire universe. It also seems quite possible that this world might have developed in a way that made me a carpenter or a dentist. Leibniz occasionally refers to novels and legends to make his point. The stories of King Arthur may not have been possible given the actual order of this world, but there seems to be nothing inherently contradictory about a world in which they could happen. Hobbits may have been precluded by the way evolution actually happened, but it certainly seems possible that things could have evolved differently. This claim that other worlds are possible may seem true but trivial. When joined with the principle of sufficient reason, though, the possibility of different worlds proves that the reason for the existence of this particular world must be sought outside the world itself. The existence of this particular world is contingent, so there must be some reason to explain why it exists rather than some other particular world. That question cannot be answered by the world itself. In Leibniz's hands, the principle of sufficient reason along with the possibility of other worlds proves both the existence and nature of God.

II. THE EXISTENCE OF GOD

Leibniz nicely summarizes this proof for the existence of God in the *Theodicy*. We can analyse it step by step:

> *God is the first reason of things*: for such things as are bounded, as all that which we see and experience, are contingent and have nothing in them to render their existence necessary, it being plain that time, space, and matter, united and uniform in themselves and indifferent to everything, might have received entirely other motions and shapes, and in another order. (T 127)

What renders this particular world contingent is the fact that other worlds are possible. Leibniz emphasizes that, at the very least, it would be possible for this world to be arranged differently in time and space. For example, the stars could trace different paths across the sky (AG 191). The argument continues: 'Therefore one must seek the reason for the existence of the world, which is the whole assemblage of *contingent* things, and seek it in the substance which carries with it the reason for its existence, and which in consequence is *necessary* and eternal' (T 127). The sufficient reason for the contingent world we experience must come from something which exists not as one of several possibilities, but as the only possibility. That is, its non-existence must be impossible, which means its existence is necessary, or as Leibniz puts it, it carries with it the reason for its own existence. This move from contingency to necessity is not quite the same as the claim that there must be a *first* cause. Even if this world had no beginning, running in a chain of causes to infinity, it would still need a reason why it was this particular infinite chain of causes. Leibniz gives the example of a geometry book that was copied from a previous book, which was copied from a previous book, and so on. Even if that chain of copies went infinitely back in time, we would still need a reason for the particular content of that book (AG 149). Leibniz continues the argument above to show not only that God exists but also what God must be like:

> Moreover, this cause must be intelligent: for this existing world being contingent and an infinity of other worlds being equally possible, and holding, so to say, equal claim to existence with it, the cause of the world must needs have had regard or reference to all these possible worlds in order to fix upon one of them. This regard or relation of an existent substance to simple possibilities can be nothing other than the *understanding* which has the ideas of them, while to fix upon one of them can be nothing other than the act of the *will* which chooses. It is the *power* of this substance that renders its will efficacious. Power relates to *being*, wisdom or understanding to *truth*, and will to *good*. (T 127)

This necessary being must provide the sufficient reason for this world, which means first of all that it must have some way to bring together and grasp all the possible worlds. The only way to conceive this process of comparison and judgement is if God understands all these worlds simultaneously. In addition, something must explain how God chooses one of these worlds, which means God must have will. Finally, something must explain why that chosen world actually comes to exist, which requires that God have power. Leibniz's analysis of God relies on this traditional division of God into three aspects – understanding, will, and power. The argument continues: 'And this intelligent cause ought to be infinite in all ways, and absolutely perfect in *power*, in *wisdom*, and in *goodness*, since it relates to all that which is possible. Furthermore, since all is connected together, there is no ground for admitting more than *one*' (T 127–8). In order for God to provide a sufficient reason, God must understand all possibilities and then be able to choose and actually create any of them. Thus all three aspects of God must be perfect or infinite, that is, they must extend to all that is possible.

This argument based on the principle of sufficient reason is the main proof Leibniz uses to establish the nature and existence of God. He occasionally goes so far as to say that if one denies the principle of sufficient reason, then there is no way to demonstrate the existence of God (NE 179). Nonetheless, in the *New Essays*, Leibniz says that there are many proofs for the existence of God, and that all of them can be made to work with some corrections (NE 438). These other proofs help illustrate the nature and role of God in Leibniz's philosophy. In the *Monadology*, he includes two other proofs. The first has come to be known as the 'ontological argument'. It was first articulated by Anselm but became prominent in the early modern period largely through Descartes' use of it in his *Meditations on First Philosophy*. The argument begins with the fact that we can demonstrate necessary properties from certain ideas. For example, from the very concept of a triangle, we can demonstrate that its angles must add up to 180 degrees and that in a right triangle, the square of the hypotenuse must equal the sum of the squares of the other two sides. These properties are necessary because to lack them would be contradictory and thus impossible. Moreover, this knowledge is *a priori*, relying only on the ideas themselves rather than experience. We know such properties as necessary and certain even if we never experience a perfect triangle and even if no such triangles have ever existed. This kind of knowledge applies to ideas outside of mathematics as well, as we can deduce necessary properties from the idea of substance or the idea of justice. If, as we did with the triangle, we analyse the idea of God – a most perfect being – we also find necessary properties. For example, by analysing the concept of a most perfect being, we find that it necessarily includes omniscience and omnipotence. Analysis also shows that the very idea of a most perfect being must include existence as one of its properties. To exist is more perfect than to not exist, so maximum perfection must include existence. Consequently, existence must be a necessary property of God just as the angles of a triangle must equal 180 degrees. Thus God must exist.

We do not need to go into a detailed examination of this argument, but it is important to note two things about its role in early modern thought. First, although it was widely taken as proving the existence of God, its main role was rather to demonstrate one property of God, namely, that God's existence is necessary, a property essential for maintaining the principle of sufficient reason. Second, there was a general sense that the proof needed some additional support. Thus Descartes only uses it after he has established that God is good and not a deceiver. Spinoza only uses it after he has demonstrated that existence is a necessary property of substance. Leibniz's criticism of the proof comes out of his criticism of Descartes' use of clear and distinct ideas, which will be examined further in chapter 4. Leibniz points out that we must be careful about which ideas we analyse, because we sometimes have notions of things that are in fact impossible, that is, notions which are contradictory. Any demonstrations that follow from such a concept are, of course, not truly demonstrated. Leibniz's point is that the very idea of a most perfect being may be contradictory, as the concept of fastest speed or largest circle would be. For the ontological argument to work, we must prove that God is possible, that is, that the idea of a most perfect being is not inherently contradictory. Leibniz seems uncertain about whether or not we can prove this *a priori*. In some places he says we cannot but we can reasonably assume it (AG 237–8; NE 437–8); in the *Monadology*, he says that the concept of a being with no limits could not be contradictory and so must be possible (M 45; AG 218). Even there, though, he appeals to other proofs. In fact, the importance of this argument for Leibniz lies not so much in proving that God exists, but in showing that if God exists (as proven by the principle of sufficient reason), then God's existence must be necessary (T 410). If God's existence is necessary, then we need no further reasons to explain it; it provides its own sufficient reason by the very fact that its opposite is impossible.

The third argument which Leibniz gives in the *Monadology* is based on the existence of necessary truths and their dependence on God's understanding. As with the ontological argument, this proof functions as much to tell us about God and our relationship to God as it does to prove God exists. If we think again about the idea of the triangle, it seems that the truths we derive from it are independent of our imagination. That is, we do not make up the fact that its angles total 180 degrees; we discover it. In this way, the truths of mathematics differ from things we just imagine, such as unicorns. In a letter to Simon Foucher, Leibniz writes, 'This possibility, impossibility, or necessity (for the necessity of something is the impossibility of its contrary) is not a chimera we create, since we do nothing more than recognize it, in spite of ourselves and in a consistent manner' (AG 1). Because we *discover* rather than *invent* them, the properties of a triangle must be true even before any person articulates them. Leibniz captures this point when he refers to these as 'eternal truths'. Necessary truths also seem independent from the existence of particular things in the world. The properties of a triangle do not depend on any perfect triangles actually existing. We see this point clearly with more complex figures, like a chiliagon: a polygon with one thousand sides. We can demonstrate truths about this chiliagon even though we have never seen one and cannot even picture one. If these truths then are independent of our mind and of contingent things, what kind of existence do they have? In the *Monadology*, Leibniz draws this conclusion – '[I]f there is reality in essences or possibles, or indeed, in eternal truths, this reality must be grounded in something existent and actual, and consequently, it must be grounded in the existence of the necessary being, in whom essence involves existence, that is, in whom possible being is sufficient for actual being' (M 44). If eternal truths are real, they must be grounded in a God who exists necessarily. Since these truths are real, God must exist.

Leibniz appeals to one other way for proving the existence of God, based on the apparent order and perfection of the world. Pointing to the laws of physics, he says,

> They do not spring entirely from the principle of necessity, but rather from the principle of perfection and order; they are an effect of the choice and wisdom of God. I can demonstrate these laws in divers ways, but must always assume something that is not of an absolutely geometrical necessity. Thus these admirable laws are wonderful evidence of an intelligent and free being, as opposed to the system of absolute and brute necessity, advocated by Strato and Spinoza. (T 332)

What Leibniz means by perfection will be considered in detail in the following sections, but his basic point is that the degree of order in the world can only be explained as the result of a being that deliberately prefers order. For Leibniz, this argument from the order and beauty of the world does not constitute a full proof for God's existence. He admits that it is possible the order came randomly, although it is so unlikely as to be practically impossible (A IV, 4, 2268). Leibniz also admits that this world does not seem perfectly good or ordered, so that we could not infer an absolutely perfect being from it. Nonetheless, of all the arguments for the existence of God, Leibniz appeals to this one as most natural, claiming that the wonders of nature lead people to think of a higher being by a natural feeling or instinct (NE 75–6). This natural feeling explains why people in many cultures have an idea of something divine. This movement from the order of the world to God also emphasizes the importance of science, which reveals the hidden order and principles behind the variety of natural phenomena.

III. THE NATURE OF GOD

We have now seen various arguments Leibniz uses to establish God's necessary existence. To fulfil the requirements of the principle of sufficient reason, though, Leibniz must not only show that God exists necessarily but also that God necessarily exists and acts in a way that sufficiently explains this particular world. In other words, even knowing that a necessary being created this world, a persistent questioner might still ask, 'But why did that necessary being choose *this* particular world?' To maintain the principle of sufficient reason, Leibniz cannot simply respond that this world exists because God chose it. He must explain *why* God chose it. This explanation relies on the relationships among God's understanding, will, and power. We can begin, though, by examining the positions that Leibniz opposes. The first position claimed that the existence of this particular world was necessary, not contingent. Thus this world explains its own reason, since any other world would be impossible. The second position claimed that this world is the result of a choice by God, but that God's choice was undetermined and arbitrary. This kind of choice was sometimes referred to as coming out of *indifference* or *equipoise*, meaning that there were no reasons tipping the balance toward one choice or another. Leibniz's position is a middle ground between absolute necessity and arbitrariness, a middle ground he calls 'moral necessity'. This middle ground is reflected in the laws of physics:

> [T]his great example of the laws of motion shows with the utmost clarity how much difference there is between these three cases, to wit, firstly an absolute necessity, metaphysical or geometrical, which may be called blind, and which does not depend upon any but efficient causes; in the second place, a moral necessity, which comes from the free choice of wisdom in relation to final causes; and finally in the third place, something absolutely arbitrary, depending upon an indifference of equipoise, which is imagined, but which cannot exist, where there is no sufficient reason either in the efficient or final cause. (T 334)

The laws of nature illustrate this middle ground because they are not absolutely necessary, since we can imagine other possible worlds with different laws, yet they reflect more order than can be explained by chance. For Leibniz, natural laws reflect the fact that the foundation of the world is a selection of what is most orderly, harmonious, and abundant.

Leibniz associates the view from necessity primarily with Spinoza (T 234). In the *Ethics*, Spinoza argues that everything which exists exists by necessity; those things which do not exist are thus impossible.[1] This view follows from Spinoza's emphasis on divine power. If this power is truly absolute then it must produce everything that is possible. If something were possible but not actually produced, God's power would be less than it could be. If everything that exists is necessary, then the properties of any person, such as what they eat for breakfast, follow with the same necessity as the properties of a triangle, which is why Leibniz sometimes calls it 'geometrical necessity'. This claim that the world itself is necessary has several radical consequences in the context of Christian thought. First, like all events, human actions are absolutely determined, a fact which undermines traditional conceptions of responsibility and freedom. Second, absolute necessity overturns any view of this world or God as good, as it makes the criterion for existence *possibility* rather than *goodness*. That is, if something is possible it must exist, whether or not it is good, orderly, or harmonious. Third, this view eliminates the need for God by eliminating this world's need for a sufficient reason. Spinoza embraced all three of these conclusions, but Leibniz vehemently rejects them, both because they overturn traditional views of God and more importantly because, according to Leibniz, they eliminate the foundations of morality. We have already seen Leibniz's main counter-argument, based on the possibility of other worlds. More specifically, his argument relies on the concept of *compossibility*, that fact that many things which are possible in themselves cannot possibly exist together, that is, are not compossible. For example, the order of things which brings about my existence as a philosopher is possible, as is the order of things which would bring about my existence as a carpenter, but these two orders are not compossible. Either can exist, but they cannot exist together. If not all possible things are compossible, then the claim that everything which is possible exists must be false. Some possible things must be excluded because they are not compatible with other equally possible things; thus there must be a reason why this particular set of possibilities exists. For Leibniz, because not all possibilities can exist together, there must be some choice between possibilities and the explanation for the existence of this particular world must lie outside the realm of contingent existence.

The alternative to necessity is arbitrariness or chance. In Leibniz's time, few argued that the world itself arose by chance. The more common claim was that the world was created by God but that God's choice was radically free and not determined by reasons. Leibniz takes this position more seriously and his response is more complex. He associates it primarily with Descartes but also with Hobbes. At first glance, the claim that God acts arbitrarily seems scandalous in a Christian context, as it seems to undermine God's goodness, but it responds to one of the first problems people pose when they begin to think philosophically about God – if God *must* be good, then God is not free, since he cannot choose anything other than the good, and God is not omnipotent, since he has no power to do bad things. More specifically, if we say that the notion of justice is necessary, then God has no choice about it or power over it. Rather, God seems subject to this notion of justice, which limits his power and even his will. Such a view seems to create some free-standing realm of ideas which are higher than God and which God must obey. Spinoza makes this point with particular clarity:

For they seem to place something outside God, which does not depend on God, to which God attends, as a model, in what he does, and at which he aims, as at a certain goal. This is simply to subject God to fate. Nothing more absurd can be maintained about God, whom we have shown to be the first and only free cause, both of the essence of all things, and of their existence.[2]

The claim that God's choices are arbitrary thus attempts to give priority to God's infinite power and free will. There were a number of ways to explain how God might still be considered good on this view. In the *Theodicy*, Leibniz distinguishes three different positions:

All these three dogmas, albeit a little different from one another, namely, (1) that the nature of justice is arbitrary, (2) that it is fixed, but it is not certain that God will observe it, and finally (3) that the justice we know is not that which he observes, destroy the confidence in God that gives us tranquility, and the love of God that makes our happiness. (T 237)

Leibniz groups these positions together because they all allow that God is not constrained by human concepts of justice and thus, at least from a human perspective, they allow God to act arbitrarily. Fundamentally, all three positions attempt to reconcile God's goodness and God's power by redefining what goodness means. On the first view, God is good but God himself chooses what counts as good.[3] On this view, God creates everything, including the concept of justice. As the first position follows from giving priority to God's will, it came to be called 'Voluntarism', from the Latin *voluntas*, which means will. Leibniz most associates this position with Descartes and it is sometimes referred to as 'Cartesian Voluntarism'. The second view allows that God happens to be good but that God could just as well choose to be bad. It is not that God *does* bad things but rather that in some real sense God *could* do them. To claim otherwise is to claim that God can only will one thing, placing limits again on God's freedom and power. The third view allows that God is good but not in the same way that human beings label things as good.

Leibniz's first response is to point out that all three attempts to reconcile God's power or will with God's goodness in fact eliminate God's goodness, replacing it with what he calls 'despotic power'. Take torturing innocent people as an example of what we consider evil. On the first view, torture is evil but only because God chose to define good and evil that way. God could just as well have made torture count as good, in which case we would all call it good and praise God for it. As Leibniz points out, this equates 'goodness' with 'whatever God wants'. Furthermore, we cannot properly praise God for being good if we would equally praise God for torturing innocent people (T 236). We would in fact only be praising God's infinite power, something more like flattery than real praise. On the second view, God happens to be good, but that is not his fundamental nature since he could just as well choose to be bad. The third position runs into similar problems. If by God's goodness we do not mean what we consider good, then we are really uttering a meaningless phrase. More specifically, we know that kindness is part of our idea of goodness, but if this tells us nothing about God's goodness, then it could just as well be that God does torture innocents, because that is what good means as applied to him. We have no way of knowing.

All three views of God have disturbing consequences for ethics. If our conception of good differs from God's, why should we obey it? More disturbing, what if we find out on judgement day that what good means for God is torture? We could find ourselves in Hell for having not tortured enough people. The problem with the other positions is slightly different, because both allow for an accessible standard of justice that is either arbitrary or not necessarily followed by God. This gives some objective status to goodness right now, but it is not something we can rely on in the future. If what counts as good is arbitrarily chosen by God, God could always change that standard. We need not suppose a temporal God who changes his mind; God might dictate that every so often the standards will change, perhaps for the sake of variety. That means that while right now kindness is good, the standard could change so that kindness becomes bad, in which case we might end up being punished for what is now good (T 237). We might respond – that wouldn't be fair! – but that is precisely Leibniz's point. If what counts as fairness does not bind God but is chosen by God, we can make no absolute appeal to it. Leibniz's arguments show that a theistic view which makes morality subject to God rather than making God subject to morality ends up looking pretty terrifying. Leibniz says that such a God cannot really be distinguished from an evil being:

> There is nothing to prevent such a God from behaving as a tyrant and an enemy of honest folk, and from taking pleasure in that which we call evil. Why should he not, then, just as well be the evil principle of the Manicheans as the single good principle of the orthodox? At least he would be neutral and, as it were, suspended between the two, or even sometimes the one and sometimes the other. (T 237; cf. T 95)

The problem is not just one of God's morality or the reliability of a just afterlife. For Leibniz, justice and goodness are objective concepts that have a necessary and universal meaning in exactly the same way as mathematical concepts. This claim is the foundation of Leibniz's ethical and political theory. Leibniz defines justice:

> Justice is charity or a habit of loving conformed to wisdom. Thus when one is inclined to justice, one tries to procure good for everybody, so far as one can, reasonably, but in proportion to the needs and merits of each: and even if one is obliged sometimes to punish evil persons, it is for the general good.[4]

The foundation of justice is helping everyone and working for the common good, that is, charity or love. Our effort, though, must take into consideration what other people deserve. Leibniz believed that we do and should take this concept as objective, which requires that it be truly universal, applying even to God. Thus he frequently associates the claim that justice depends on the will of God with a political claim – that justice is determined by the decisions of those who control a state. Both ultimately define justice in the same way, as whatever is pleasing to those with the greatest power. With such a concept of justice, we lose any possibility for criticizing those with power. Leibniz describes its consequences:

If that were true, there would never be a sentence of a sovereign court, nor of a supreme judge, which would be unjust, nor would an evil but powerful man ever be blameworthy. And what is more, the same action could be just or unjust, depending on the judges who decide, which is ridiculous. It is one thing to be just and another to pass for it.[5]

The problem of the universality of concepts in relation to God goes beyond moral and political issues. The concept of justice is just an example of the status of essences or ideas in general. The 'Voluntarist' position claims not only that the essence of justice is arbitrarily created by God but that the essence of something like a triangle is similarly created and thus could be different. For example, God could have made the hypotenuse of a right-angled triangle equal the sum of the sides rather than the square root of the sum of their squares. To deny this possibility is to subject God to essences rather than essences to God. The fact that human beings cannot really conceive such a triangle might be merely a consequence of the way God created human minds. Leibniz points out that this position really means that there are no *necessary* truths, since in a strict sense God could have made them differently. Their apparent necessity is really just a psychological limitation on what we can think. While we might now accept this psychological necessity as sufficient, the same argument about justice applies here – if these truths are arbitrary then God could change them. Such a view renders necessary truths and thus all reasoning fundamentally uncertain.[6] These problems show that what is at stake in the issues around God's will is not just the goodness of the world but also the foundations of reason.

Thus far, Leibniz's arguments rest on the unappealing consequences of freeing God from the constraints of morality. Leibniz's primary counter-argument rests on his conception of the will. He defines the will: 'one may say that *will* consists in the inclination to do something in proportion to the good it contains' (T 136). To will is necessarily to will *something*. To will is to choose and to choose means to choose some option. In fact, the will cannot really be separated from what is willed; it is just a dynamic inclination toward it. The Voluntarist position must posit a will in God that has no objects but rather creates those objects; it is a will which chooses without having anything to choose from.

Beside the fact that such an act is incomprehensible, it is simply not what we mean by will or choice. Rather, it is sheer randomness. From the very conception of the will, then, it follows that the objects of the will must precede it. Thus the attempt to free God's will from the constraints of justice do not succeed in elevating God's will but rather eliminate it, replacing it with sheer randomness. This randomness is precisely what makes such a God so terrifying. Leibniz also thinks it is obviously wrong:

> But, as I have declared more than once, I do not admit an indifference of equipoise, and I do not think that one ever chooses when one is absolutely indifferent. Such a choice would be, as it were, mere chance, without determining reason, whether apparent or hidden. But such a chance, such an absolute and actual fortuity, is a chimera which never occurs in nature. All wise men are agreed that chance is only an apparent thing, like fortune: only ignorance of causes gives rise to it. (T 310)

While perhaps not all wise men agree that chance is a fiction, to claim that God acts without reason is to deny the ultimate validity of the principle of sufficient reason, which is one of the two foundations for all knowledge. If we admit chance into the very foundation of things, how can we not admit it into our laboratories and engineering projects? Here we see the intersection between Leibniz's concern for science and his concern for consistency – if we affirm the use of the principle of sufficient reason in the practice of science, consistency demands that God's creation of the world also have a sufficient reason. Moreover, if we allow for chance, we have no need for a God in the first place. The principle of sufficient reason is what establishes God's existence; if we allow for its violation by a God who acts arbitrarily, we might just as well allow this world itself to arise randomly.

These problems reflect one of the fundamental difficulties in thinking through the concept of God, which is that God's power and goodness inevitably conflict. We have now seen several ways in which one can sacrifice goodness to maintain power. Leibniz takes the opposite approach, so we can already see the difficulty he faces. Making the essences of things precede God's will and choice seems to make God depend on something else, namely, the ideas among which he chooses. Leibniz occasionally uses language that suggests this dependence: 'But to act rightly we must affirm alike on one side the independence of God and the dependence of creatures, and on the other side the justice and goodness of God, which makes him dependent upon himself, his will upon his understanding or his wisdom' (T 164). In other passages, Leibniz says God is not answerable to anyone else, but that he is answerable to himself, that is, to his own wisdom and goodness (T 238). Leibniz is well aware of the problems this dependence raises, but he believes they are avoided because these constraints on God's will come from the necessity of God's own nature. Pierre Bayle charged that this position subjected God to something like fate. Leibniz responds, 'This so-called *fatum*, which binds even the Divinity, is nothing but God's own nature, his own understanding, which furnishes the rules for his wisdom and his goodness; it is a happy necessity, without which he would be neither good nor wise' (T 247). On Leibniz's account, the absoluteness of God's independence is not weakened but shifts from his will to his infinite understanding.

Leibniz's account of God's understanding plays a central role in his philosophy, not only because it explains the creation of this particular world, but also because it is the foundation for the status of necessary truths and is the model for human understanding, which he says mirrors or expresses that of God. What is this understanding that God has? What does it contain? All possibilities in all possible combinations, that is, everything which can be conceived. From the principle of sufficient reason, the contents of God's understanding must be necessary – if there were ideas God could have but did not have then God would not truly be infinite or omniscient and there would have to be some external reason to explain his limits. The principle Leibniz relies on is similar to the one Spinoza uses – if it is possible, then it exists – but these possibilities exist only as ideas. Thus specific reasons are not required to explain the contents of God's understanding. It simply contains all possible ideas, and this follows from the very nature of infinite understanding. Note, though, that God has all *possible* ideas. Some thoughts are excluded. God does not have an idea of a square circle, because a square circle is impossible. Leibniz would similarly say that God has no idea of a fastest motion or a substance which is not naturally eternal, because both contain inherent contradictions which, by the principle of contradiction, make them impossible. Strictly speaking, they are not ideas at all. They not only cannot exist but they cannot even be clearly thought. There are other thoughts which are possible in themselves but not possible in certain combinations. They are possible but not compossible. So God would have an idea of me as a philosopher and an idea of me as a carpenter, but could not have an idea of one world in which I am both at the same time. Similarly, God cannot have an idea of a world in which there is variety but every individual thing is perfect, or a world in which human beings have bodies but do not make mistakes. These ideas do not exist because they are contradictory and thus impossible.

Leibniz discusses God's understanding in terms of ideas rather than propositions. This way of talking about knowledge follows from one his most important theories, referred to as the *concept containment* theory of truth. In a letter to Arnauld, Leibniz states: '[I]n all true affirmative propositions, necessary or contingent, universal or singular, the notion of the predicate is always in some way included in that of the subject – the predicate is present in the subject – or I do not know what truth is' (WF 111–12). If a property can be truly predicated of a subject, then that predicate must in some sense be part of the concept of the subject. So to say that human beings are rational is to say that the concept of 'human being' involves or includes the concept of rationality or that if you understand the concept 'human being', you must also understand the concept 'rational'. This point seems plausible and simple, but it has major consequences for Leibniz's conception of substance and of logic. Both will be dealt with in more detail later; the relevant point here is that the concept containment theory leads to a particular way of talking about the truth. Reasoning is not so much a synthetic process of putting together distinct ideas but rather an analytic process of explicating what is already contained in a particular concept. In a sense, Leibniz says that all true statements are identities. True statements say 'A is A' and their content comes simply from explicating what is already included in the subject. Leibniz talks of the mind of God as containing ideas rather than containing propositions because propositions merely explicate ideas. Ideas intrinsically contain their relations. Leibniz extends this conception of truth to all of a subject's predicates, including those we normally consider extrinsic. Thus Leibniz continues the above passage:

[T]he notion of an individual substance involves all of its events and all its denominations, even those that are completely called *extrinsic* (that is to say, which belong to it only in virtue of the general interconnectedness of things, and of the fact that it expresses the whole universe in its way) because *there must always be some foundation for the connection between the terms of a proposition, and it must be found in their notions.* (WF 112)

We have already seen the basis for this position when we considered that the sufficient reason for the existence of any particular thing must ultimately include the entire order of the universe. Fully understanding any one thing requires fully understanding the particular causes that produced that thing, and in turn the causes that produced them, ultimately including the entire universe. All these must be contained in the complete concept of that thing, which is to say that when God thinks of it, its idea also contains everything that relates to it. We can thus get some sense of the immensity of God's infinite understanding. God has not only the complete idea of each existing thing, but also complete ideas of every possible thing. These ideas are utterly determinate. God does not have an idea of me which includes the possibility of my being a carpenter or a philosopher, or an idea of Adam in which he may or may not eat the apple. Rather, God has one idea of me as philosopher, which includes the whole universe that would make that happen, and another idea of me as a carpenter, which includes a whole different universe, just as he has an idea of this particular Adam implicating this whole world and ideas of other slightly different Adams, each involving a slightly different universe. The concept containment theory means that various possible worlds can be considered in two ways. They can be thought of as the totality of substances involved in the existence of that world, or they can be thought through any one of those substances. Thus the choice to create any one substance is simultaneously the choice to create one particular world.

The ideas in the mind of God can be divided into two groups. God has an idea of every particular possibly existing thing. These ideas are grouped into various worlds or orders, each of which in itself is possible, while being incompatible with other equally possible worlds. God also has ideas whose opposites are not possible. These are necessary truths. Among these necessary truths are the basic truths of metaphysics, mathematics, and virtue. In his discussion with Arnauld, Leibniz illustrates the difference between these two kinds of ideas with the example of a sphere. From the abstract idea of a sphere, one can infer many necessary predicates, which are included in that concept. To imagine a sphere which lacked these properties would be to imagine something impossible because inherently contradictory. The concepts from which we infer necessary truths, however, are abstract and incomplete. In the same letter to Arnauld, Leibniz contrasts the concept of himself with the concept of a sphere:

> [T]here is quite a difference. For the notion of me in particular, and that of every other individual substance, is infinitely more extensive and more difficult to comprehend than a specific notion like that of a sphere, which is incomplete and does not involve all the circumstances which are necessary in practice for arriving at a particular sphere. (WF 108–9)

Because the concept of a sphere is general, all the properties derived from it are necessary and apply to all possible spheres. Leibniz calls such ideas incomplete because they remain indeterminate. They lack properties that would place them in any particular world, any particular order of existence. So he continues: 'In order to understand what myself is, it is not enough that I can feel myself to be a substance which thinks; we would have to conceive distinctly of what distinguishes me from all other possible minds, of which I have only a confused experience' (WF 109). On a general level, we can know that the idea of 'human being' includes certain predicates like thought without considering what particular thoughts a particular person will have, as we can consider the properties of a sphere without considering its size. Any possibly existing thing, though, has an infinity of properties placing it in a possible world. The concept of an actual sphere would involve whether or not it is a beach ball or a marble, what factory it came from, which children played with it, and so on, implicating an entire universe. All of these ideas, general and particular, have a kind of necessity and independence from the will of God. All exist in the understanding of God simply because they are possible.

The immensity of God's understanding follows from omniscience, which in turns follows from omnipotence. The very immensity of God's understanding, though, might undermine any commonality between human ideas and those of God. What could such a mind share with finite minds like ours? To avoid this problem, Leibniz must account for some relation between our ideas and those of God such that we can talk about God's justice without equivocation. Leibniz describes the relations between our ideas and those of God as a relation between part and whole: our wisdom is like a drop to God's ocean (T 108) or a single ray of God's divine light (AG 140). There is no difference in kind between God's ideas and ours but only a difference in quantity – we have less ideas and our ideas contain less detail. The relations between ideas are the same for us and for God: 'All reasonings are eminent in God, and they preserve an order among themselves in his understanding as well as in ours; but for him this is just an order and a *priority of nature*, whereas for us there is a *priority of time*' (T 192). The details of Leibniz's epistemology will be discussed in chapter 4, but as the complete concept of any particular thing involves an entire universe, we can never grasp that complete concept, and since the sufficient reason for the predicates of any existing thing depend on the entire universe, we can never grasp the sufficient reason for any particular thing. While God can deduce the location of my next vacation from my concept alone, I cannot. Otherwise it would be as easy to be a prophet as it is to be a geometer (WF 109). This limitation, however, does not necessarily apply to general concepts. Because such concepts are incomplete, they do not involve infinite predicates and the sufficient reason for their properties does not involve infinity. Although our grasp of these is still limited, we can deduce necessary properties from them and these properties follow with the same necessity in our minds as they do in the mind of God. Thus principles of geometry and justice apply equally to all things, human or divine.

We have seen that Leibniz's concept of will requires that the will be an inclination toward something. The object of God's will is his understanding, that is, the collection of all possible ideas. It remains then only to establish how God's will is determined, that is, which ideas are chosen. By the definition of will given earlier, the will tends inevitably toward what seems best. Since God's understanding is perfect, God's will inevitably inclines toward what is truly good. In fact, Leibniz does not give much argument for his claim that God is good. By the principle of sufficient reason, the kind of will that God has must follow necessarily from his nature as infinite. Like almost everyone before him in the European tradition, Leibniz assumes that a being with infinite power and wisdom would naturally be good. In fact, Leibniz takes 'acting wisely' to mean 'acting for the good':

> It seems that we must concede that God always acts wisely, that is, in such a way that anyone who knew his reasons would know and worship his supreme justice, goodness, and wisdom. And in God there never seems to be a case of acting purely because it pleases him to act in this way, unless, at the same time, it is pleasing for good reason. (AG 29)

Another way to look at this connection is that doing evil follows from some weakness. We do evil because we lack something we desire and we lack the power to use good means to get it. An infinite being would have no reason to do evil. This position was widely assumed and is put particularly well by Descartes:

> To begin with, I recognize that it is impossible that God should ever deceive me. For in every case of trickery or deception some imperfection is to be found; and although the ability to deceive appears to be an indication of cleverness or power, the will to deceive is undoubtedly evidence of malice or weakness, and so cannot apply to God.[7]

We could deny these points, but then we are left with a frightening view of morality. Whatever direction God's will takes, it must follow from the necessity of infinite power and wisdom. If those lead to evil rather than good, it would follow not only that God was evil but that the wiser and more powerful a person was, the more evil they should be. A commitment to morality would only follow from weakness and stupidity.

According to Leibniz, then, God necessarily wills the greatest good. He calls this a *moral* necessity, in contrast to *absolute* or *geometrical* necessity, but it is no less certain or determined (T 395). Does this mean that God's will is not free? The answer depends on what one means by 'free'. If 'free' means undetermined, then God's will is not free, but such a freedom is impossible and incoherent. To complain that God's will is not free in that sense would be like complaining that a circle is not at the same time a triangle. Moreover, to act freely is not the same as to act randomly. Otherwise the freest people would be those who acted most erratically and we would be most free when our actions made the least sense. In the context of determinism, 'free' could refer to two things. First, an action is free if it follows from one's own choice and is not compelled by someone else. As infinitely powerful, God has this freedom in the highest degree. Second, we could say that an action or choice is free when what is chosen is really what we want. So we could say that I am less free when I choose to do things that ultimately conflict with what I want, either because I choose based on feeling rather than deliberation or because I choose based on misunderstanding. As infinitely wise, God also has this freedom in the highest degree. Leibniz writes:

From this it is at the same time obvious how the Author of the World can be free, even though everything happens determinately, since he acts from a principle of wisdom or perfection. Indeed, indifference arises from ignorance, and the wiser one is, the more one is determined to do that which is most perfect. (AG 151)

In sum, by an absolute necessity, God's understanding contains all possibilities, some of which are necessary and some of which are contingent. By a moral necessity, God's will chooses the best of those options, that is, the best possible world. From God's power, that world is created. We are now in a position to see the coherence of Leibniz's use of the principle of sufficient reason. The sufficient reason for a particular existing thing like myself is the entire order of the universe which produced me. The sufficient reason for that particular order of the universe is the necessity of God's will toward the good and the necessity of the possibilities presented by God's understanding. These in turn follow from the very necessity of the existence of an infinite being. The sufficient reason for the existence of that being is provided by its necessity – it would be impossible for it not to exist. This account saves the principle of sufficient reason, but it may seem like Leibniz has tricked us. If this world follows with certainty from the nature of God, then in what sense is it contingent? Doesn't the sufficient reason make the world necessary? Leibniz's analysis is subtle. He repeatedly urges a distinction between what is determined with *necessity* and what is determined with *certainty*. The latter remain contingent because, in themselves, they are not necessary. Thus Leibniz sometimes says this world follows with a hypothetical necessity: given that God wills the best, then this world follows necessarily. This hypothetical necessity does not alter the fact that other worlds are possible and even have some kind of existence in the mind of God.

To understand the point of this distinction, we must keep in mind that the key issue for Leibniz is not what we may naturally expect it to be. We expect a discussion of necessity and contingency to focus on the opposition between free will and determinism. With this focus, all that matters is that Leibniz concludes for determinism; the difference between necessity and contingency appears irrelevant and even misleading. That kind of free will, however, is not the issue for Leibniz, as he thinks it is manifestly absurd. Leibniz's distinction between necessity and contingency makes more sense if we consider his purpose, which is to maintain both the principle of sufficient reason and the goodness of God. Views that attribute this world to an arbitrary choice by God or to absolute necessity fail on both. Leibniz's position combines and reconceives aspects of both positions, which is why he calls his position a middle between the two. Following the necessitarian position, there is a sense in which everything possible does exist, but only in the mind of God. God's understanding includes all possible worlds, not just the good ones. Non-existent possibles do have some kind of existence; even the most evil world exists as an idea in the mind of God. The fact that these possible worlds are not compossible, however, forces us to bring in God's will, drawing on the Voluntarist position. The fact that this will is determined toward the good may conflict with some of our intuitions about free will, but it does not at all conflict with God's goodness, which is Leibniz's concern. On the contrary, God can only be considered truly good if his will is determined. Otherwise, even if he happens to be good right now, he could always become evil, or just redefine what counts as good.

IV. THE BEST OF ALL POSSIBLE WORLDS

We have seen so far how Leibniz reconciles the principle of sufficient reason with God's infinite power and goodness, with the consequence that God necessarily does the best. Since God created this world out of all the other possibilities, it follows that this world is the best. That conclusion, though, throws the whole previous argument into question. Surely this is not the best of all possible worlds! One winter in Chicago should suffice to demonstrate the point. Even the happiest optimist must acknowledge that our lives could involve less pain and suffering. Hume, through the character of Philo, lists four specific ways that the world could be improved; for example, animals could be motivated to action by variations in degrees of pleasure rather than by pleasure and pain, or nature could operate by rules that were less general and supported the good, so that, as he puts it: 'A fleet, whose purposes were salutary to society, might always meet with a fair wind. Good princes enjoy sound health and long life. Persons born of power and authority, be framed with good tempers and virtuous dispositions.'[8] Well before Hume, Pierre Bayle referred to Alfonso, King of Castile, who supposedly said that if God had consulted him when creating the world, he could have suggested some improvements (T 248). The problem is not just that we suffer more than necessary but also that the suffering is not fairly distributed. Even if people often get what they deserve, we all see good people who live difficult lives and bad people who flourish. Cancer pays no regard to the moral character of its victims. Heaven and Hell ease the problem somewhat, and Leibniz himself says that the only way to maintain divine justice is to allow for punishment and reward in an afterlife. Even so, a system with no justice until after we are dead hardly seems best.

The existence of moral evil, as opposed to just physical suffering, raises a further set of problems. In one sense, the problem is not as severe, since we can blame moral evil on the person who does it while we cannot blame a hurricane for the suffering it causes. Yet if God created this world and all the people in it, he must bear some responsibility for the bad that people do. At the very least, God allows evil people to exist and to harm the innocent. A powerful God could eliminate them sooner or at least limit their power. Furthermore, if God is all-knowing, then he must know that these people will do evil even before he creates them and the world which produces them. Yet he creates them anyway. On a view which embraces the principle of sufficient reason, in which all things including evil actions follow exactly from determinate causes, the problem is even greater. God creates a world in which some people are determined to do evil. This appears unfair to those who suffer from those evil actions, but it even appears unfair to the ones who commit those evil actions, who end up in eternal Hell for doing something they were determined to do. Leibniz's account of the will adds even more problems. All people have the same will: all will what seems best. People who do evil actions, then, do not exactly want to commit evil but rather are so confused as to see evil as good.

These problems are different aspects of what has come to be known as the 'problem of evil'. Leibniz summarizes the problem clearly in the *Theodicy*:

> [O]ne cannot deny that there is in the world physical evil (that is, suffering) and moral evil (that is, crime) and even that physical evil is not always distributed here on earth according to the proportion of moral evil, as it seems that justice demands. There remains, then, this question of natural theology, how a sole Principle, all-good, all-wise and all-powerful, has been able to admit evil, and especially to permit sin, and how it could resolve to make the wicked often happy and the good unhappy? (T 98)

The problem of evil has a long history in the tradition of Western thought, going at least back to Epicurus. Probably the greatest statement of the problem is David Hume's *Dialogues Concerning Natural Religion*, published posthumously in 1779, but the problem came to prominence in Leibniz's time largely through the writings of Pierre Bayle. Bayle delighted in sceptical arguments and one of his favourites was the problem of evil. The core of his position was that reason conflicts with the truths of Christianity, forcing one to choose between reason and faith. Although his explicit conclusion was that one must choose faith, his repeated arguments against Christian principles made him controversial and threatening. For Leibniz, a philosopher committed to both reason and the existence of a good God, Bayle's position posed a grave threat. The *Theodicy* takes Bayle as its primary target and main interlocutor. It remains one of the greatest attempts to reconcile faith and reason and to neutralize the problem of evil.

The problem of evil can be taken as a conflict between three propositions:

(1) There is an all-powerful being who creates this world.
(2) That being is perfectly good.
(3) This world is not perfectly good.

Any two of these propositions can be held together, so one can avoid the problem by denying any one of them. If this being is not all-powerful, then we can affirm its goodness and explain imperfection in the world by saying that this was just the best that being could do. One such attempt to limit God's power is to claim that God does not create the world from nothing (*ex nihilo*) but rather must work with some independent and imperfect material. A more radical response is to posit two gods, one good and one evil, allowing for a good god who lacks total power over the world. The imperfections of the world would be attributed to the evil god. This position was associated with Manicheanism; Pierre Bayle argues that it is false but is the most reasonable view of the world. A second approach is to maintain that God is all-powerful but deny that God is perfectly good. While this might seem shocking in a Christian context, we have already seen one attempt to do this, which is to argue that God does what is best but that what 'best' means for God is not what it means for us. That is, both God and the world are not good in the way we human beings define goodness.

The third option is to deny proposition (3) and argue that this really is the best world. Leibniz is famous for making this argument and its apparent implausibility has done the most to generate an image of him as a naïvely optimistic philosopher. In fact, Leibniz's argument depends on qualifying all three propositions. He qualifies God's power by limiting it to the realm of possibility. God cannot create *any* world, because some of them are impossible. This world is the best *possible*, because any better world we could imagine would be found to contain inherent contradictions. Leibniz also qualifies the second proposition. Although he maintains that goodness and justice have the same meaning for us and for God, he argues that we mistakenly identify the good in terms that are too anthropocentric. We take good to mean what is good *for us*. God's goodness has a broader scope, directed not only toward human beings but toward the whole order of the universe and each thing in it. We must consider both of these qualifications in order to see how Leibniz can plausibly dispute the third proposition and argue that this really is the best of all possible worlds.

First, what does Leibniz mean by 'good' and 'evil'? The status of evil has always posed a problem for Christianity. If evil exists and if God creates all that exists, then God must create evil. Yet why would a perfectly good being create evil? Leibniz's answer has its roots in Greek thought, but became central in the philosophy of Augustine and then in Descartes. Augustine saw the existence of evil as the greatest intellectual obstacle to belief in Christianity; he himself was initially drawn toward Manicheanism. Augustine's solution to the problem was to say that, strictly speaking, evil does not exist. Evil literally is nothing. This is not to say that there is no suffering and no murderers, but these result from limitations of being and goodness, not from a positive evil force.[9] The point is that human beings are not part evil and part good, but rather just a limited amount of goodness. Thus two causes – one for good and one for evil – are not required. We only need a cause for good, which is God. In a dialogue on freedom, Leibniz has one character charge, 'To account for sin there must be another infinite cause capable of counterbalancing the influence of divine goodness.' The other character, representing Leibniz's own view, responds that there is such a cause, but that it is nothingness. He explains, 'The Platonists and Saint Augustine himself have already shown us that the cause of good is positive, but that evil is a defect, that is, a privation or negation, and consequently, it arises from nothingness or nonbeing' (AG 114). Evil is a privative concept, representing not a thing but rather a lack of a thing. An example commonly used to illustrate this is the concept of darkness. We could think of a dimly lit room as composed partly of darkness and partly of light, in which case we would explain it by looking for two causes, one producing darkness and one producing light. Such an approach, however, is misleading, because darkness is a privative concept, referring only to a lack of light. The dimness of the room cannot be blamed on the force of darkness but only on the lack of light. Thus its cause is only one – light – but given in a limited amount. Leibniz takes evil to be like darkness and good to be like light. What we would call evils in the world are not a mixture of two positive forces but only a reflection of differing degrees of goodness. Consequently, evil needs no positive cause. Leibniz says, 'the formal character of evil has no efficient cause, for it consists in privation' (T 136). This approach does not solve the problem of evil, but it shifts the key question. Rather than ask – why does God create evil? – the question is, why does God make limited or imperfect things? The latter question is easier to address.

Can evil really just be explained as a privation of good? In the *Theodicy*, Leibniz distinguishes three kinds of evil: 'Evil may be taken metaphysically, physically, and morally. *Metaphysical evil* consists in mere imperfection, *physical evil* in suffering, and *moral evil* in sin' (T 136). Metaphysical evil refers simply to finitude, to the fact that things are limited. Metaphysical evil must exist in any possible world, because the only unlimited thing is God. If God is to create anything, limitation must be part of that creation. On this level, we can see clearly that a finite amount of being or perfection does not require two sources, one for what we have and one for what we lack. All being and perfection comes from one source, but it comes in limited amounts. Metaphysical evil gives rise to physical evil. Because we are limited, we can be harmed. Our bodies get sick and eventually die. We feel cold. We desire things we lack. All of these sources of suffering follow from the more basic fact that we are finite. Given Leibniz's account of will, in which evil and error come from lack of understanding, metaphysical evil also explains moral evil. Our understanding of things is limited and so we make mistakes. Some of those mistakes lead us to act in ways we would describe as evil. These actions, though, simply result from our finitude, from the limits of our finite minds. This evil does not need two causes, one to explain what we understand and one to explain the understanding we lack. All of our understanding and perfection comes from God, but it comes in limited amounts.

As with evil, the foundation of goodness or perfection is metaphysical. If evil is nothing, then perfection is being. Insofar as anything exists, it is good; insofar as it has limited existence, it can do and suffer evil. This connection between being and perfection is already implicit in Leibniz's view of God. The ontological argument claims that an infinite, perfect being must exist, because to exist is more perfect than to not exist. Moreover, we have seen that God, an infinite being, must be perfectly good. If so, then evil follows only from limitation. Leibniz ties these claims together in the *Monadology*. He first argues that God has no limits and contains as much reality as possible. He continues:

> From this it follows that God is absolutely perfect – *perfection* being nothing but the magnitude of positive reality considered as such, setting aside the limits or bounds in the things which have it. And here, where there are no limits, that is, in God, perfection is absolutely infinite. It also follows that creatures derive their perfections from God's influence, but that they derive their imperfections from their own nature, which is incapable of being without limits. (M 41–2; AG 218)

The equation between being and perfection draws further support from the very fact that anything exists. Although God exists by necessity, it would not be impossible for God to create nothing, to create no world at all. Yet things do exist, so there must be some reason why being overcomes nothing. Whatever the details of this reason, it must be better to exist than to not exist.

Leibniz takes one other perspective on this point, emphasizing that it is the very nature of being to strive for existence. This connection follows a tradition of linking being to action or power, perhaps clearest in Spinoza's equation of being with power and striving or *conatus*, a term Leibniz also uses. The connection appears in Leibniz's claim that force belongs to the basic nature of any being, a claim that will be examined in the next chapter. Leibniz takes this perspective in the essay, 'On the Ultimate Origination of Things:'

> [S]ince something rather than nothing exists, there is a certain urge for existence or (so to speak) a straining toward existence in possible things or in possibility or essence itself; in a word, essence in and of itself strives for existence. Furthermore, it

follows from this that all possibles, that is, everything that expresses essence or possible reality, strive with equal right for existence in proportion to the amount of essence or reality or the degree of perfection they contain, for perfection is nothing but the amount of essence. (AG 150)

Here, the reality contained by possibilities gives them some claim to exist. Passages like this seem to conflict with Leibniz's more anthropomorphic descriptions of God's choice for creation of the world. Here, creation seems more like an automatic process where possibilities exist in God's understanding and the combination which contains the most reality overpowers the others and comes into existence. Nonetheless, the phrase 'with equal right' points again to a God who necessarily chooses according to what is just and good. If perfection equals being, then the maximization of perfection should also be the maximization of being. Thus the above passage concludes: 'From this it is obvious that of the infinite combinations of possibilities and possible series, the one that exists is the one through which the most essence or possibility is brought into existence' (AG 150).

The maximization of being seems quite different from what we normally recognize as good, and Leibniz's account risks making the goodness of God too different from our own. The most common way that Leibniz describes the criteria of perfection, however, comes a bit closer to our intuitions. In the *Monadology*, he equates perfection with 'obtaining as much variety as possible, but with the greatest order possible' (M 58; AG 220). In the *Theodicy*, he defines perfection as 'infinitely simple and uniform, but yet of an infinite productivity' (T 255). In the *Discourse on Metaphysics*, he says that the most perfect world 'is at the same time the simplest in hypotheses and the richest in phenomena' (DM 6; AG 39). On one side is order, simplicity, and uniformity. On the other is variety, productivity, and richness. Leibniz usually supports and explains this criterion with analogies: one who acts perfectly is like a geometer, who can find the best construction for a problem; like an architect, who makes the best possible use of his resources; like a householder, who uses his resources so that all is productive; like a machinist, who acts in the least difficult way; like an author, who includes the greatest number of truths in the smallest volume (DM 5; AG 38–9). Leibniz's model is largely aesthetic: his most frequent models come from music and architecture, both pointing toward the pleasure we find in harmony. The most basic model Leibniz appeals to, however, is that of science and the natural world. A good scientific explanation explains the most phenomena with the fewest principles. The perfection found in scientific accounts mirrors the perfection of nature itself, where a few simple laws generate the whole variety of nature.

Leibniz justifies this criteria of perfection partly by appeal to our own aesthetic appreciation of harmony and diversity, but it rests logically on the need to maximize being. He assumes that maximizing *quantity* of being means maximizing *variety* of being. This connection was common in Christian thought before Leibniz. If variety of being is good, and if variety requires variations in levels of limitation, then metaphysical evil can be justified in the name of variety. The connection between variety and order is less clear, but some of Leibniz's analogies already point toward it. In examples such as the geometer or author, order appears merely aesthetic, but in others, order is required for maximum effect. For example, for the householder to maximize production, his limited resources must be used in an orderly, systematic way. The architect must act efficiently in order to use limited resources for the fullest effect. In other words, if means are limited, then maximization of being requires a simplicity and order in the means for producing it. To some degree, these analogies break down in relation to God, since God does not have limited resources to maximize. Leibniz explains in the *Discourse on Metaphysics*:

> It is true that nothing costs God anything – even less than it costs a philosopher to build the fabric of his imaginary world out of hypotheses – since God has only to make decrees in order that a real world come into being. But in matters of wisdom, decrees or hypotheses take the place of expenditures to the extent that they are more independent of one another, because reason requires that we avoid multiplying hypotheses or principles, in somewhat the same way that the simplest system is always preferred in astronomy. (DM 5; AG 39)

Although nothing 'costs' God, what God creates must work within certain constraints, namely, the limits of the possible. Because not all things are compossible, maximizing creation requires minimizing contradictions. The way to do this is to maximize order so that each thing integrates with all others. Leibniz continues the above passage from the 'Ultimate Origination of Things':

> In practical affairs one always follows the decision rule in accordance with which one ought to seek the maximum or the minimum: namely, one prefers the maximum effect at the minimum cost, so to speak. And in this context, time, place, or in a word, the receptivity or capacity of the world can be taken for the cost or the plot of ground on which the most pleasing building possible is to be built, and the variety of shapes therein corresponds to the pleasingness of the building and the number and elegance of the rooms. (AG 150)

Leibniz's view of space and time will be discussed later, but both represent possible orders of existing things. Space is the order of things coexisting and time is the order of things existing in succession. Thus the capacity of space and time refers to limits of compossibility, the limits of what can exist at the same time and in the same causal chain. This limitation requires that variety combine with order. A continuum offers a good model of the maximization of variety and order. One the one hand, every possible degree of being and degree of difference exists, while on the other hand, movement in one part of the continuum effects the whole, assuring that each part is ordered to all the others. This is just what Leibniz thinks this world – the best possible – is like. In sum, because something exists, it must be more perfect to exist than not to exist. Because God does what is most perfect, he must create as much as possible. Anything that is not contradictory is possible. Therefore, God creates a world in which the most things can exist without contradiction, which requires a world as orderly as possible. Perfection demands both the greatest variety and the greatest order.

Given Leibniz's conception of evil as lack, the problem of evil becomes a problem of limitation. Leibniz's criterion of perfection serves to justify limitations, by setting up a conflict between the perfection of the whole and the perfection of the parts. God's goodness is directed toward the whole, which maximizes being by maximizing order and diversity. The perfection of any single part can be sacrificed for at least three reasons: for the sake of variety, for the sake of order, for the sake of other parts. Since God is the only infinite being, any thing that is created will have limits and thus will involve metaphysical evil. To create the most variety, these things must vary in the kinds of limits they have and in the degree of limitation, which is to say that variety requires that things be more and less perfect (T 142). Leibniz occasionally argues that variety requires a continuity of degrees of perfection, with some thing for every degree of perfection. As he puts it, there is no vacuum of forms (T 131). We human beings seem to be near the top of this progression, but it would be arrogant to assume that we are the pinnacle of created perfection. Leibniz frequently mentions angels as more perfect beings, and even hypothesizes that there might be rational beings on other planets who are more perfect than us (T 330, 337–9). On a general level, we recognize that this kind of variety of perfection is good; as Leibniz says, no one would complain that all rocks do not sprout flowers or that all ants are not peacocks (T 278). Our hesitancy comes from wishing we were a little higher in the hierarchy, but if we recognize the goodness of ants in spite of their limitations, we can hardly complain about our position. Few of us would wish to trade places with ants *or* peacocks. Second, the good of one part can conflict with the requirement for order. Order requires that parts be treated in regular ways, and the simpler the order, the more likely it is to conflict with the unique needs of particular parts. Leibniz gives the patterns of weather as an example. The global weather system is an excellent example of a few simple principles generating a wide variety of phenomena over space and time, but this entails that not every place will get the appropriate weather all the time. Leibniz says: 'Shall God not give the rain, because there are low-lying places which will be thereby incommoded? Shall the sun not shine as much as it should for the world in general, because there are places which will be too much dried up in consequence?' (T 206). We can see how Leibniz's shifting of the criterion of perfection away from human concerns and toward order anticipates the suggestion of Philo mentioned earlier – if the weather always favoured the good, this might be better for human beings but it would mar the overall order and perfection of nature. Finally, the good of the parts cannot be fully separated from the good of the whole, so God must have some regard for the parts. The good of one part sometimes justifies limitations in other parts. So Leibniz writes:

> No substance is absolutely contemptible or absolutely precious before God. ... It is certain that God sets greater store by a man than a lion; nevertheless it can hardly be said with certainty that God prefers a single man in all respects to the whole of lion-kind. Even should that be so, it would by no means follow that the interest of a certain number of men would prevail over the consideration of a general disorder diffused through an infinite number of creatures. This opinion would be a remnant of the old and somewhat discredited maxim, that all is made solely for man. (T 188–9)

We began by laying out the problem of evil as a conflict between three propositions. While Leibniz does not deny that God is good, his discussion of perfection shifts the meaning of goodness away from the biased, anthropocentric way we usually take it. This shift makes the claim that this world is the best possible much more plausible. Even if we take regard for the whole of creation, though, this conception of metaphysical good seems distant from our own ideas of goodness. What about kindness? What about justice? Leibniz cannot accept a fully non-anthropocentric conception of the good, but he struggles to account for why human beings are special. In a letter to Arnauld, Leibniz writes it must be the case:

> That intelligences, or souls capable of reflection, and of knowledge of eternal truths and of God, have many privileges that exempt them from the revolutions of bodies. That for them moral laws have to be combined with physical ones. That everything is done primarily for these intelligences. That together they make up the republic of the universe, of which God is the ruler. (WF 136)

Leibniz justifies our special status partly through our similarity to God. In the *Discourse on Metaphysics*, he writes:

> Since God himself is the greatest and wisest of all minds, it is easy to judge that the beings with whom he can, so to speak,

enter into conversation, and even into a society – communicating to them his views and will in a particular manner and in such a way that they can know and love their benefactor – must be infinitely nearer to him than all other things, which can only pass for instruments of minds. (DM 35; AG 66)

Leibniz's anthropomorphism here sounds a bit silly, as if God prefers those he could sit down and have a beer with, but Leibniz's God has no desires and does not need people for company or for praise. The philosophical foundation of Leibniz's position comes down to two points. The first is that God does not regard all parts as equal but shows more concern for those that are more perfect. Human beings are more perfect, even in the metaphysical sense of producing the most effects through the simplest means. Leibniz adds that human perfections are peculiar in that they conflict the least with each other and in fact assist each other. The more perfect a person is, the more they contribute to perfecting others (DM 36; AG 67). The second is that our perfection brings human beings to the level of self-consciousness. We act according to deliberate reasons and our actions remain part of our identity and memory. We have a conscious concern for our future. These traits render us susceptible to reward and punishment in a way that trees, rocks, and even animals are not. In other words, the demands of justice apply to us, but not to them. The essence of justice exists through the necessity of God's understanding, which requires that creatures like us – those that make choices and bear responsibility – get what they deserve. From an individual perspective, this difference can be good or bad, depending on our own actions. Animals and trees do not get to experience Heaven, but they also need not fear Hell. In any case, the best possible world must fulfil two requirements: it must maximize the metaphysical good of variety and order and must meet the demands of justice, that is, moral good. Leibniz calls these two demands the order of nature and the order of grace:

Here there is no crime without punishment, no good action without proportionate reward, and finally, as much virtue and happiness as possible. And this is accomplished without disordering nature (as if what God prepared for souls disturbed the laws of bodies), but through the very order of natural things, in virtue of the harmony pre-established between the kingdoms of nature and grace, between God as architect and God as monarch. Consequently, nature itself leads to grace, and grace perfects nature by making use of it. (PNG 15; AG 212)

In sum, Leibniz approaches the problem of evil by addressing each of its three aspects, not just by denying that this world is imperfect. While he does not back off from his claim that God is good in the same sense as we conceive goodness, he does interpret goodness or perfection in a way that makes it easier to reconcile with the sometimes difficult realities we experience in this world. Similarly, Leibniz places limits on God's power. If God truly has infinite power, why must he sacrifice the good of the parts for the sake of the whole? If God can do anything, why can't he make a world with order and variety in which all the parts are happy and good? Leibniz's answer is that, in a sense, God cannot do *anything* but can only do what is *possible*. God's understanding contains all possible worlds and this one is the best of them, but many other worlds are impossible because they contain intrinsic contradictions. We might vaguely imagine a world with variety and all perfect parts, but if we were to think it through clearly, we would find such a world impossible. Variety necessarily requires limitations. Thus to say that this is the best possible world is to say that any better world would be impossible. These require-ments, in a sense, limit God's power, but the limitations are not imposed on God from outside but by the very nature of God's own understanding. Keeping in mind that evil is not something positive but only a manifestation of limitation, Leibniz says that while earlier thinkers have placed the origin of evil in matter or in necessity, the ultimate origin of evil is the inherent limitations of things as understood in God's mind:

It can be said that it arises from the very essences or natures of created things; for the essences of things are eternal, even though things aren't. It has always been true that three times three is nine and it will always be so. These things do not depend on God's will, but on this understanding. ... God's understanding is the source of the essences of created things, such as they are in him, that is, bounded. If they are imperfect, one can only blame their limitation on their boundaries, that is to say, the extent of their participation in nothingness. (AG 115)

Among all the worlds contained in God's understanding, many contain evil and the kind of quasi-existence this evil has is independent of God's will. In a sense, we can still say that the inherent evil in the essences of these possible worlds is caused by God, but not by his will. God's will only comes into play in choosing to create the best of these worlds. In this choice, God only wills what is good, but that choice requires also the existence of some evil. Leibniz distinguishes God's relation to the two by saying that God wills what is good but only permits what is evil (T 136–7).

Leibniz's account appears coherent but it still stretches the limits of belief. Could it really be that any improvement would either render this world impossible or actually cause more harm than good? A world without cancer seems both possible and better, but Leibniz must deny this. To understand his position, we must consider the basic structure of his argument. Leibniz combines confidence in deductive *a priori* arguments with scepticism about *a posteriori* conclusions from experience. Hume himself acknowledges the effectiveness of this approach, claiming that if one has an *a priori* reason to believe this world is good, then experience cannot disprove it.[10] Leibniz argues for exactly this position. The principle of sufficient reason proves that God exists, is good, and creates the best possible world. Thus this world must be the best possible. The relevant question then is not if this world *seems* to be the best but if experience *proves* that it is not. Leibniz summarizes the two sides of his position: 'It is thus that, being made confident by demonstrations of the goodness and the justice of God, we disregard the appearances of harshness and injustice which we see in this small portion of his Kingdom that is exposed to our gaze' (T 120). Scepticism about human knowledge plays a key role in Leibniz's argument. This scepticism takes two main targets. The first is our inability to judge whether or not a given world is possible. To know if a certain world contained contradictions, we would have to grasp an infinite interconnection of causes, which is impossible. The contradictions are too often hidden from the reach of a finite intellect. Thus although we might imagine a better world, we cannot analyse that world to judge its possibility. Thus such imagined worlds cannot *prove* that this world is not the best possible. This point is all that Leibniz needs, but he goes on to suggest some reasons why such worlds might not be possible. More concretely, he suggests that it would be impossible for a world to have less suffering and not be worse in other ways. We have already seen how less suffering here might be worse for the rest of the universe, but Leibniz argues that it might be worse even for us. We need variety; all pleasure all the time would bore us:

> Indeed, the most distinguished masters of composition quite often mix dissonances with consonances in order to arouse the listener, and pierce him, as it were, so that anxious about what is to happen, the listener might feel all the more pleasure when order is soon restored, just as we delight in small dangers or in the experience of misfortune for the very feeling or manifestation they provide of our power or happiness, or just as we delight in the spectacle of ropewalkers or sword dancing for their very ability to incite fear, or just as we ourselves laughingly half toss children, as if we were about to throw them off. ... On that same principle it is insipid to always eat sweet things; sharp, acidic, and even bitter tastes should be mixed in to stimulate the palate. He who hasn't tasted bitter things hasn't earned sweet things, nor, indeed, will he appreciate them. Pleasure does not derive from uniformity, for uniformity brings forth disgust and makes us dull, not happy: this very principle is the law of delight. (AG 153)

Pain draws attention to pleasures we might otherwise take for granted, as we often do not appreciate good health until we get sick (T 130). Moreover, the greatest pleasures come from overcoming obstacles and from making progress, so that suffering often improves us and brings us pleasure in the long run. Thus if we were to experience only pleasure – one of the ways that Hume's character Philo suggests that the world could be better – our lives might in fact be less good. We must be careful again to see the point of these arguments, which is not to prove *a posteriori* that any different world would be impossible or worse. That knowledge is beyond human reach. The goal rather is to undermine the opposite argument. We all recognize that pain is sometimes necessary; given the infinite complexity of the universe, how can we judge that any of the suffering it contains is unnecessary?

On one side, then, Leibniz argues that a world with less suffering would either be less good or impossible; on the other side, he argues that our world might have less suffering than it seems. His argument is simple and plausible:

> Thus since the proportion of that part of the universe which we know is almost lost in nothingness compared with that which is unknown, and which we yet have cause to assume, and since all the evils that may be raised in objection before us are in this near nothingness, haply it may be that all evils are almost nothingness in comparison with the good things which are in the universe. (T 135)

We know there are other planets in our solar system and we have reason to think that every star is like our sun and could have its own planets. We don't know what life is like in any of those places. Our temporal limits are just as great as the limited space we occupy. Judging from the small part we know would be like judging the perfection of a painting while only looking at a tiny fragment of it (AG 153). Moreover, we have reason to think there is goodness and order that we do not perceive. We see perfection whenever we are able to consider something in nature as a whole:

> Such a whole, shaped as it were by the hand of God, is a plant, an animal, a man. We cannot wonder enough at the beauty and contrivance of its structure. But when we see some broken bone, some piece of animal's flesh, some sprig of a plant, there appears to be nothing but confusion, unless an excellent anatomist observe it: and even he would recognize nothing therein if he had not before seen like pieces attached to their whole. (T 207)

The solar system is another example of a relatively whole piece that exemplifies order and diversity. Science repeatedly finds order in what previously seemed irregular (AG 192). Leibniz again uses the example of the solar system, which was one of the things Alfonso suggested he could have helped God improve. If the solar system was the irregular and complicated system described by Ptolemy, the only system known to Alfonso, perhaps it could have been improved. What we now know and Alfonso did not know was that that irregularity came from our limited understanding, not the solar system itself, which the Copernican theory shows to be a model of perfection (T 247–8).

In making these sceptical arguments, Leibniz must maintain a delicate balance. Pushed too far, they render God's goodness completely inaccessible to finite minds like ours. To maintain the ability to meaningfully say that God is good, Leibniz must maintain that we know what goodness is and that this concept of goodness applies equally to God and human. We can know that this world maximizes order and variety, just as we can know that good people must eventually be rewarded. If we knew that God violated these principles, we would have the capacity to say that God was not good. The limitations of our experience do not threaten this knowledge, which is *a priori* and based on necessary truths, but only limit our ability to judge *a posteriori* how well this particular world fits these criteria. Further, we are able to apply these criteria to the world, with limits. We have already seen Leibniz's claim that when we are able to grasp part of nature as a relative whole we can see its perfection. We see this most clearly in Leibniz's rehabilitation of 'final causes'. Final causes refer to the purpose for which something happens: to explain an event by its final cause is to explain the motivation or end for which it occurred. For example, to explain the construction of a house by appeal to someone's goal of having a place to live, is to explain it by its final cause. One characteristic of the early modern period is a firm rejection of final causes. All things should be explained by efficient causes, which meant that things should be explained in terms of the properties of matter and the laws of physics. For example, why is an eye able to gather light? If we reply, it gathers light so that it can see, then we are appealing to final causes. If we instead reply by explaining the characteristics of the tissue composing the eye and the laws by which light moves, then we are appealing to efficient causes. For the 'new science', appeals to final causes were seen as empty and inappropriate. As a scientist, Leibniz is fully committed to explanation in terms of efficient causality, but he is unusual in allowing some role for final causes. His primary concern is with maintaining God's goodness. In the *Discourse on Metaphysics*, he writes strongly, 'I advise those who have any feelings of piety and even feelings of true philosophy to keep away from the phrases of certain extremely pretentious minds who say that we see because it happens that we have eyes and not that eyes were made for seeing' (DM 19; AG 52–3). Leibniz takes the rejection of final causes as a threat to love of God, but final causes also have practical uses in guiding scientific investigations. If one assumes that nature is designed according to the criterion of perfection, that is, that the natural world maximizes order and variety, one can more easily discover the laws by which the universe works. Leibniz gives anatomy and optics, as well as his own discovery of the conservation of force, as examples in which the assumption of perfection has helped people to focus their investigations (DM 21, 22; AG 53–5). Leibniz occasionally uses final causes to support his arguments. Explanations that show nature's perfection are more likely to be true. For example, Leibniz believes that his account of substances, which will be examined in the next chapter, would best maximize order and variety. This fact in itself lends support to his theory. Similarly, Leibniz relies on our sense of justice to argue that the unbaptized cannot simply be condemned to Hell. That would be unjust and so we can be sure God would not do it. Our ability to apply our concept of goodness to God and this world also has an important role in ethics. Like God, we should strive to maximize perfection. Our limited perspective means that sometimes will we strive for things that seem to contribute to the world's perfection but in fact do not. Nonetheless, if we had no idea at all of the world's perfection, we would never know how to act. Leibniz explains that since we know this is the best possible world, we must accept whatever has happened as ultimately being for the best. We do not know, though, what will happen in the future. Leibniz writes,

Toward the future, however, he [the moral person] struggles with the highest enthusiasm to obey God's mandates, either expressed or presumed from the public consideration of the divine glory and benevolence. And when in doubt he does that which is more prudent, more probable, and more conducible; just as a lively and industrious man, full of enthusiasm, acts to make his things good, if a great prince has destined him to negotiate with another. (A VI, 4, 2379)

To approach the world using final causes is to work with the assumption that things happen in the most perfect possible way and that our role is to increase the world's perfection, maximizing harmony and diversity. The actual perfection of the world will remain largely unrecognizable, but it is not utterly so.

Leibniz's discussion of the best possible world does not deny the reality of the suffering and evil we experience. He is not a naïve optimist, living in denial or lost in ideas. His defence of the world primarily is a criticism of those arrogant enough to condemn the world based only on their limited experience. Yet there remains a life-affirming core to his position. He argues that historians and misanthropes have exaggerated the evils of human life. Life has more pleasure than pain, but we take many pleasures for granted. When Bayle claims that history is a record of abuses and points to the number of prisons we have, Leibniz responds by pointing out that we still have many more houses than prisons (T 216). He states this affirmation clearly:

Had we not knowledge of the life to come, I believe there would be few persons who, being at the point of death, were not content to take up life again, on condition of passing through the same amount of good and evil, provided always that it were not the same kind: one would be content with variety, without requiring a better condition than that wherein one had been. (T 130)

Leibniz believes most people would make this choice. At the same time, he also reconfigures where we should seek pleasure. As with most philosophers, he takes intellectual pleasure as the highest and most stable, referring particularly to the pleasures of science, which consist most directly in finding the hidden order behind diverse phenomena. The pleasure of science and philosophy cannot be separated from the pleasure that comes from the contemplation and love of God. We cannot truly love God, he says, unless we love God's creation, which is this world. Love of God is thus mediated through love of the beauty we find in the order of nature. Finally, knowing that this is the best possible world does not free us from the suffering we encounter in this little part of it, but knowing that our suffering is necessary and contributes to the greater good makes it easier to bear. Knowledge that this world is the best and was created by a good God allows us to accept what happens not just with a sense of Stoic resignation to the inevitable but with a genuine contentment.

CHAPTER 3

SUBSTANCES

I. SUBSTANCE IN EARLY MODERN PHILOSOPHY

For Leibniz, the basic constituents of the world are simple substances, which he later famously calls 'monads', based on the Greek word *monas*, meaning *one*. In making substances the basic constituents of reality, Leibniz follows the dominant position in Western philosophy up to his time. The theory of substance is one way of responding to what seem to be two undeniable aspects of human experience. On the one side, we experience almost constant change and interaction, but on the other side, we naturally pick out and talk about individual things that maintain some identity through change. In theorizing the basic nature of being, that is, in establishing an ontology, one can take change as primary, in which case independent things reduce to relatively stable patterns of change, or one can take things as primary, in which case change reduces to properties belonging to individuals. We can generally call the former a process ontology and the latter a substance ontology. 'Substance' then is really just a technical term for 'thing'. One distinctive aspect of European philosophy, in contrast to Indian or Chinese philosophy, is that it maintained a substance ontology for so long. This substance ontology is intimately linked to Christianity, in which God must be maintained as fundamentally distinct from the world, that is, as a separate substance rather than part of a broader all-encompassing process. Similarly, if I can spend eternity in Heaven or Hell, then I must exist fundamentally as an individual, both so that I can maintain the same identity in such radically different circumstances and so that I can be held solely responsible for my actions. We see this connection in Spinoza, where the attempt to redefine the role of substance is inseparable from a broader attack on the basic metaphysical views of Christianity. As Leibniz's strangest and most counter-intuitive claims follow from his theory of substance, before considering his position it will be helpful to first consider the context in which it emerges.

Substance has traditionally filled two interconnected functions, going back at least to Aristotle. Primarily, substance is a means of individuation. We are able to look at the world as separate things – to individuate things – because they are individual substances; what we call a thing aligns with what is truly a substance. For substance to maintain this function of individuation, it must have three properties. First, it must have some independence which allows us to separate it from other things. Second, it must have some unity, which allows us to call it *one* thing rather than an aggregate of things. Third, it must have some permanence or stability over time, which allows us to call it the same thing through change. The second function of substance is as the subject of predicates or the thing which has properties. This use of substance partly follows from the structure of Indo-European languages. When I say, 'the coffee is bitter', I seem to distinguish coffee from bitterness. The coffee is the thing, the substance, and is basically what is real. The bitterness is a quality of that substance and thus its reality or being depends on that substance. So 'bitter' in itself has a kind of incompleteness; it must be the bitterness of some thing. In the terms of early modern philosophy, bitter is a *mode* of a substance. This belief that qualities cannot be fundamental beings but only aspects of substances is a deep assumption running through most of Western philosophy. Most early modern philosophers – even Spinoza – do not seriously consider the possibility that the world might just consist of an interplay of qualities. The distinction between a subject and its predicates or a substance and its modes intersects the role of substance in individuation. Any thing designated as a substance will have multiple properties. To maintain some unity behind these properties, one must posit a being which is in some sense independent of these properties, a unitary thing which has a multiplicity of properties. Similarly, all qualities change over time. To maintain the stability of a substance over time, substance must be seen as something other than its qualities, as a thing which had those qualities but now has these.

For Aristotle, a substance is some material shaped or formed in a distinct way. This table is a substance because it consists of wood cut into this particular shape. It differs from other tables because it consists of different matter (that is, it is a different piece of wood) and it differs from chairs both by its matter and its form. This view of substance is called hylomorphic, from *hyle* meaning matter (originally wood) and *morphe* meaning form. The meaning of form, though, goes beyond just shape. Aristotle takes form as the function of a thing, so that a substance is some amount of matter shaped to have a coherent function. The table can be considered a substance not only because of its shape but because it has a function, a function that both depends on and explains its physical shape. Finally, form can be taken as action; it points not just to function but to functioning. Matter, in contrast, lacks inherent action. Matter is passive and represents potentiality, because it can be shaped into many different forms and activated in many functions. A tree is a paradigmatic substance. Why do we tend to consider a tree one thing, rather than a collection of things (leaves, branches, bark, etc.) or part of a broader thing (a forest, ecosystem, etc.)? For Aristotle, a tree is one thing because it consists of a certain amount of material functioning in a coherent way, generating a particular shape, all directed toward one function: its own survival and growth. Its form is that functioning itself, the very process of living. Thus the form of a human being is not so much our shape but the very activity of living, including eating, perceiving, and thinking. Two points follow from this view of substance, both of which were widely rejected in the early modern period. First, although this view has a kind of dualism of form and matter, these lack independent existence. A form is matter formed or acting in a certain way. Matter also cannot exist but with some form. Thus neither matter nor mind are themselves substances but rather they are two aspects of substance. Consequently, one cannot give an account of the material world simply in terms of matter; one must use form as well. Second, taking form as function necessarily connects it to a purpose. To function is to function for the sake of something, toward a goal or *telos*, as the tree functions in order to maintain itself, grow, and reproduce. Explaining the material world in terms of form, then, leads to explaining it in terms of final causes. We have already seen how appeals to final causes were widely rejected in early modern physics.

Early modern philosophy is characterized by a shift away from the Aristotelian conception of substance, which dominated Scholastic medieval philosophy. The new model of substance is rooted in Descartes. His famous discussion of a piece of wax in the second meditation makes this new model fairly clear. He begins with a cold piece of wax, listing its qualities – it is hard, yellow, sweet, etc. When the wax is heated, all of those qualities change. It becomes soft, clear, tasteless, and so on. All of its qualities change through this process, yet we still call it the same piece of wax, the same thing. We take it as a substance, meaning it is fundamentally distinct from other things, it has a unity that makes it one thing, and it remains the same thing over time. These require some separation between the substance itself and the qualities it has at any particular moment. In Descartes' terms, this distinction is one between substance and its modes or modifications. The same analysis appears in his discussion of the human mind. I find myself thinking a wide range of thoughts, yet I consider myself to remain the same thing. The varying and multiple thoughts are the 'modes' of the one substance which is my mind. The modes change but the substance remains the same; the modes are multiple but the substance is one.

This Cartesian conception of substance proved extremely unstable, running into conflict with other dominant trends in early modern thought. The first problem is on the level of epistemology. One characteristic of early modern thought is a shift in priority from examining what exists to examining the limits and nature of human knowledge, that is, a shift from the primacy of metaphysics to the primacy of epistemology. Before making claims about reality, one must first examine how the human mind comes to know reality. As philosophy became more and more concerned with the limits of human knowledge, particularly the root of human knowledge in experience, it became less and less tenable to claim that the basic constituents of reality were substances. The reason for this conflict is obvious. Qualities – which are all we ever experience – have characteristics which are exactly the opposite of those of substances. Qualities are always changing and multiple. An emphasis on experience makes it difficult to claim that the fundamental nature of reality is exactly the opposite of what we experience. This problem is most clear in the development of 'Empiricism', which is the view that all knowledge comes from experience. While John Locke, the clearest representative of Empiricism, does not reject the concept of substance entirely, he does claim the term has no real meaning because it cannot be derived from experience. He calls it an 'I know not what', which we assume behind experience. Locke thus eliminates any direct role for substance in the process of individuation, since individuation must be based on experience.[1]

The other threat to substance came from the attempt to give a scientific account of the physical world, which required giving an account of all physical things in the same basic terms. The terms were those of efficient causality, conceived as the collision of matter. The tendency of science at the time was not only to reject any appeal to purposes in explaining the material world, that is, to final causes, but also any appeal to substance itself as an explanatory principle. To explain the difference between a tree and a dog by appeal to the natures of tree-substances and dog-substances was seen as non-explanation, amounting only to reasserting that the two are different. A true explanation relies only on the basic nature of matter and the general laws of motion. The physical world began to be viewed as composed of homogeneous stuff, matter, configured in different ways by the basic laws of motion. Following this line of thought, it was easier to view the being of the tree and the dog as lying not in substance but merely in relatively stable configurations of matter. This line of analysis tends to push substance to one of two extremes. Substance can expand to become the whole of the material world, leaving only one substance and making what we call things particular configurations of its modifications. This position is clearest in Spinoza, but Descartes himself is led to it as a view of the physical world. The other alternative is for substance to shrink and become the simplest constituents of the physical world, atoms. This was a common view in the early modern period, derived from Epicurus and made prominent by Pierre Gassendi, one of the leading intellectuals in the seventeenth century. On either view, substance loses its function for individuation. What we normally call things, like trees and dogs, become either modifications of one substance (nature) or aggregates of a multitude of substances (atoms). The being of a dog or tree thus lies not in being a substance but in being a particular arrangement of something common. The breakdown of the role of substance in individuation is more difficult to apply to minds. We might accept one of these accounts of the material world but still maintain that each of our minds is a distinct substance. Such a view, however, raises grave problems for the relation of mind and body – what relationship can a unitary substantial mind have with a body composed of atoms? Such a view also runs counter to the general desire for a unified science, since it leaves reality divided into two radically different kinds, one of modifications or aggregates of physical substance, the other as a multiplicity of distinct, unitary mind substances. Thus we find Spinoza arguing that minds are not substances but only modifications of an infinite mind, while others argued that there are no minds at all but only this material reality.

II. THE SIMPLICITY AND UNITY OF SUBSTANCE IN LEIBNIZ

Leibniz's account of substance emerges in the context of this broader crisis, a crisis made more urgent by the intimate connection between a substance ontology and the metaphysics of Christianity. Leibniz appears as one of the great defenders of the idea of substance, but the development of both science and philosophy in his time made it difficult to return to either the Cartesian or Scholastic conception. Like his account of God and the creation of this world, Leibniz takes elements from both Descartes and the Scholastics, again attempting to reconcile philosophy and religion. This reconciliation leads to two of his strangest claims – that substances do not interact and that bodies are not substances but only well-grounded phenomena. The basis of Leibniz's conception of substance is that the three basic properties of substance – unity, independence, and identity through change – must be all or nothing. If substance is only partly independent, then the substance cannot be truly taken as an individual. Changes in that substance would be partly explained by other substances, in which case the substance should not be taken as an individual but rather as a part or aspect of a broader process. Similarly, if a substance only has a temporary stability, then its creation and continued existence must be explained by the broader order of nature, in which case again, it is not a true individual but rather a part or aspect of nature. To maintain the concept of substance, then, Leibniz claims that substances are independent of everything but God, that substances have an absolute unity that entails having no parts, and that substances have an absolute persistence over time, existing since the beginning of the universe and lasting for eternity. For Leibniz, a rigorous thinking through of the concept of substance leads to a view of the world as composed of separate substances, each existing eternally and independently, with no interaction between them.

The arguments Leibniz uses to establish the existence and nature of substances cannot be separated from his physics. In fact, these arguments provide one of the best examples of how he uses his expertise in other areas to support and develop his philosophical views. The core of his argument focuses on the need for true unities as the foundation of reality. Anything which is an aggregate, that is, which is composed of parts, derives its reality from the reality of its parts. Leibniz uses an army as an example of an aggregate. We can talk about an army as a thing, we can analyse it and write books about the nature of armies, but whatever properties an army has come only from the people composing it. The reality of an army depends entirely on the reality of its constituent parts. Even properties most easily attributed to the army itself, like its power and organization, can be reduced to the actions of the individuals who compose it. Put simply, without people, the army does not exist. Thus an army is not something real in itself but rather is a convenient way of talking about an aggregate of parts, which are real. The problem is that this analysis applies to the parts of the army as well. Human beings, taking them only as living bodies, are also aggregates. The body is composed of parts – flesh, blood, bones, and so on. Once again, the properties of the body, such as the ways it functions as a whole, can be reduced to the properties of its various parts. Thus the reality of the body derives from its parts. It's not just that without a heart the body would die; if you removed all of its constitutive parts, the body would not exist at all. Thus like the army, the body seems to lack its own reality and seems to just be a convenient way of talking about an aggregate of parts. This analysis of parts into further parts can continue indefinitely. The bones are themselves composed of molecules, without which they would not exist, and the molecules also have parts, and so on. The problem is that, if every aggregate derives its reality entirely from its parts, without which it would not exist, then we are led to two options. Either our analysis will stop at some basic component which is not an aggregate and does not itself have parts, or else we will have to conclude that aggregates in the physical world are utterly unreal. In other words, if things have any reality at all, they must be composed of or derived from substances which are true unities, perfectly simple, and without parts. Leibniz summarizes this point:

> So every machine also presupposes some substance in the parts of which it is made, and there is no multitude without true unities. To cut the point short, I hold as an axiom the following proposition which is a statement of identity which varies only by the placing of the emphasis: nothing is truly *one* being if it is not truly one *being*. It has always been held that *one* and *being* are reciprocal things. (WF 124)

Leibniz was by no means the first to address this problem. He criticizes two common attempts to resolve it. The first relies on material atoms. If we continue to divide material things into parts, and those parts into further parts, at some point we might reach minute, simple bodies that cannot be further divided. These atoms would not be aggregates because they cannot be divided into parts. Their unity means that their reality is their own, not derived from what composes them. They would be true substances and all other material things would be aggregates of them. The unity of these atoms would thus ground the reality of the aggregates they form. That is, the reality of things like armies, bodies, and bones would lie in their being ways of talking about collections of real atoms. Leibniz criticizes physical atoms for several reasons, but his strongest argument is that anything which exists in space is divisible. In practice, some bodies might be so hard or small that we lack the technology to divide them, but that lack does not make them true unities. Anything that takes up space has dimensions, has a length, so we can imagine a line cutting that length in half. Our inability to actually make that cut does not matter. Thus the claim that atoms are true unities appears to be merely an assertion, supported empirically only by the limited sharpness of our knives. This problem with atoms led to the second main alternative, grounding extension in mathematical points. A mathematical point by definition has no dimensions. In a sense, a point exists in space but does not itself take up space. Since a point has no length or breadth, it is not divisible and cannot be considered an aggregate. It thus has the required unity, but it falls into a different problem. If a point truly lacks dimensions or takes up no space, then points can never be added together to compose something extended across space.

These problems come from the nature of a continuum. Leibniz frequently refers to two great problems of human understanding, calling them the two 'labyrinths'. One is the relationship between necessity and contingency; the other is the composition and nature of a continuum. Leibniz explains a continuum: 'When points are situated in such a way that there are no two points between which there is no midpoint, then, by that very fact, we have a continuous extension' (AG 201–2). Because there is a midpoint between any two points, any length in a continuum can in principle be divided. A continuum can be indefinitely divided: it can be divided at any point and within any section it can be divided into smaller and smaller sections (AG 251). Since a continuum can be divided, it cannot itself be a true unity or a substance, and because it is infinitely divisible it can never be reduced to indivisible parts. We could call it an aggregate all the way down, or a pure plurality. The problem with taking atoms or points as the basic constituents of the physical world can be illustrated by considering a paradigmatic continuum, a geometrical line. The ultimate constituents of a line cannot be smaller lines, because by the definition of a continuum, a line between any two points can be divided at a midpoint. No matter how small, any line can be divided, so a line cannot be the ultimate constituent of another line. In contrast, points have no length so they cannot be divided, but for this very reason they also cannot be added together to form a line. No matter how many points with a length of zero are added together, their total length will still be zero. They will not form a line. Thus a line can neither be composed of smaller lines nor of points. If the reality of an aggregate depends on its parts, and if, like a line, any continuum is an aggregate all the way down, then a continuum cannot be fully or independently real.

The problem in analysing the material world is that space is a continuum, so if bodies are defined simply by taking up space, that is, by extension, then they exist only in this continuum. But a continuum cannot be independently real. Leibniz believes that if we take space and extension across space as real entities, we find them to be incoherent – they must be composed of parts but they

cannot be composed of parts. The impossibility of deriving extension from either physical atoms or mathematical points simply
reflects the contradictory nature of a continuum. If space cannot
itself be composed of parts, we are left with two alternatives.
Either space is simply an illusion with no reality at all, or the
reality of space must derive from some true unities which do not
themselves exist in space. These must be immaterial. They are
Leibniz's monads or mind-like simple substances. Their origin in
explaining the basic constituents of reality is reflected by what
Leibniz sometimes calls them: metaphysical *points*, *atoms* of substance or formal *atoms* (AG 142, 139). The material world cannot
be literally *composed* of non-material substances. No matter how
many immaterial things you add together, you will not get a
material thing. Yet grounding reality in immaterial substances
does not necessarily leave the physical world simply an illusion.
Leibniz here uses one of his key concepts: space and extension
across space are *well-grounded phenomena*. Leibniz compares
extension to a rainbow. A rainbow is not a substance but it is also
not nothing or mere hallucination. We can analyse rainbows,
predict them, rely on them in certain ways, and talk about them
as things, because they are manifestations or expressions of real
things. Extension has a similar status for Leibniz: 'In just the
same way a rainbow is not improperly said to be a thing, even
though it is not a substance, that is, it is said to be a phenomenon,
a real or well-founded phenomenon that doesn't disappoint our
expectations based on what precedes. And indeed, not only sight
but also touch has its phenomena' (AG 182). Material things are
to the sense of touch what rainbows are to the sense of vision.
The concept of 'well grounded phenomena' must be considered
in two contexts. The first is Leibniz's doctrine of expression. We
have seen that two things express each other when the relationships between the elements in one are the same as the relationships
between the elements of the other. The relationship of expression
holds no matter how different the elements themselves are. For
Leibniz, although the material world differs radically from the
immaterial, spatial relations can still express the real relations
between substances, just as a rainbow can express the movement
of light. This relationship of expression makes both phenomena
well grounded. They can reveal truths about what they express.
The second context is Leibniz's account of human perception,

which cannot require interaction between the mind and other things. This account of perception is complex and will be explained in the following chapter, but in basic terms, space is the way that finite minds perceive the infinity of individual monads. For Leibniz, space expresses the relationships between coexisting things, while time expresses the relations between things that do not all exist at once. The important point is that the relationship of expression is not between the physical world and the world of immaterial monads but between the perceptions of one mind – which appear as organized in space and time – and the rest of the world. Their existence in the human mind rather than as independent beings is what makes space and time *phenomena*.

This denial of the ultimate status of the extended physical world seems strange and might appear to sacrifice science to the needs of metaphysics. Leibniz sees it rather as a reconciliation of physics and metaphysics. Metaphysics demands that reality consist of true unities. Physics, however, best explains the physical as an infinitely divisible continuum. We have already seen how the attempt to give a unified account of all physical things in terms of the collision of matter tended to undermine the individuation of things in terms of substance. Analysis in terms of physics works best by explaining all material things as aggregates. As long as one forces the metaphysical requirement for unity into the world of physics, one will necessarily limit physical analysis. The attempt to generate a unified science will fail, since most physical things will be accounted for as aggregates while others (such as atoms) will not. As much as we might associate Leibniz with monads, his account of the physical world runs to the opposite extreme. In physics, analysis should stop at no parts; everything should be further analysed, no matter how small or unified it may seem. By moving the principle of unity outside the material world, Leibniz can give a unitary account of the physical world through motion and collision within a continuum, accounting for all phenomena as aggregates. We see here one of the reasons why Leibniz's philosophy is so difficult to interpret. At the same time that he defends one of the most extreme versions of a substance ontology, he is also one of the first European philosophers to give a thoroughly process account of both the physical world and, since human beings perceive the world through space and time, of human experience. We see the anti-substance side of Leibniz's philosophy in an exchange of letters between Leibniz and Arnauld, in which Leibniz in effect argues *against* appeals to substance or unity in the physical world. Arnauld suggests that some physical things might have intrinsic unity, for example, that we might designate a material thing as one thing because it has a kind of cohesion in space. Leibniz responds by asking Arnauld to imagine two diamonds now in different parts of the world (WF 117–18). We might label them 'a pair' of diamonds, but they clearly do not make a unitary substance. If those two diamonds are brought closer together, this proximity does not somehow unify them into one substance. Even if they are attached together, they remain two things. Thus proximity and cohesion in space do not suffice for true unity. Arnauld suggests another possibility, coherence in function. A tree might be a unitary substance because it operates in a coherent, self-maintaining way over time. Leibniz again offers a counter-example. If coherence in function counts as a unified substance, then the agents of the Dutch India Company should form one substance, even though they are spread all over the world (WF 127). But no one would consider them one true substance. If we suggest both proximity and coherent function, Leibniz gives us the example of a bunch of sheep tied closely together (WF 118). They act in a coherent way and are next to each other in space, but clearly do not form one substance. The point of all these examples is that if we are going to give an account of the material world, then we must account for it entirely through patterns of aggregation. In fact, 'thing' becomes a relative term:

> That is to say, it is more appropriate to think of them as one thing, because there are more relations between the ingredients. But in the end all these unities derive their completeness only from thoughts and appearances, like colours and other phenomena which we nevertheless continue to call real. (WF 126)

The unity we attribute to material things – and thus anything in our perception – is only a matter of convenience, relative to our own perceptions and concerns. The split between extension as phenomenal and substances as real thus allows Leibniz to give a coherent view of reality while allowing for physical descriptions of the world that do not directly appeal to substance for explanation.

This split, however, does not make substances irrelevant. At the very least, the order and transformations in substances are what make the extended world a *well-grounded* phenomenon rather than simply an illusion. Analysis in terms of physics gives us true information about the real world and the substances that compose it.

The second element of Leibniz's argument against extension as the fundamental reality of the physical world comes from his account of force. The conception of the physical world Leibniz criticizes took the essence of physical things as simply extension across space. From extension, one can get shape and size (a configuration of space with certain dimensions), position (relationships between things in space), and motion (change of position over time). We have already seen the first problem with this account, that space is not fundamentally real. Given the status of space as ideal, it already follows that there will be something phenomenal or ideal about motion, and Leibniz frequently mentions matter and motion together as examples of well-grounded phenomena. More specifically, if the basic property of physical things is only extension in space, then motion can only be change of position over time. With this conception of motion, two conclusions follow, both of which suggest that motion is not ultimately real. The first is that motion only exists over time (AG 118, 135, 163). To say that my cup moved from the desk to the floor is to say that its position – its distance from the desk and its distance from the floor – changed over a certain interval of time. Without that interval of time, motion seems not to exist, because at any given point, the cup simply is a certain distance from the desk and the floor. In the next moment, those distances will change, but at any one moment, it seems that the cup is not moving. This observation has led to problems going at least back to Zeno's paradoxes, but for Leibniz, the issue is that motion is not a property of the cup itself.[2] It is a description of a situation over time, not a property of any of the things involved in that situation. If reality consists of things and their properties, and motion is neither a thing nor a property of a thing, then motion cannot be real. This point leads Leibniz to move from motion to force, which is a real property and can exist in a given moment: 'As for motion, what is real in it is force or power; that is to say, what there is in the present state which carries with it a change in the future. The rest is only phenomena and relations' (WF 207). Leibniz's second argument supports this same move to force. If motion is just change of position in relation to other things, then there is no way to determine which things are actually moving (DM 18; AG 131). That is, if motion is just the change in the distances between the cup, desk, and floor, then we can just as easily say that the desk and floor are the things that have moved. We would find that description strange, but only because of our limited perspective. Imagine a ship pulling out of port and a person walking at the same speed across the deck toward land. From the perspective of the watchers on shore, the ship moves and the person is stationary. From the perspective of the passengers on board, the person moves across the deck. We might appeal to the perspective of the land as the true one, but imagine that the ship is heading west at around a thousand miles per hour. Those on shore would say it is moving very fast, but someone on the sun would see it as stationary while the earth itself rotated. The point again is that motion itself does not seem to be a property of any thing. To be real, it must express some other property. Both arguments suggest that motion must be grounded in force (DM 18; AG 51).

It is important not to exaggerate the problem of the reality of motion. If we allow that there are set laws of motion, then the relativity of motion has little effect on physics as a science. In Leibniz's terms, motion is a *well-grounded* phenomenon. He holds strongly to the modern view that all physical phenomena must be directly accounted for only in terms of motion and collision. In fact, he argues that one test for any law of motion is that it should apply just as well no matter which body is taken as the one moving (AG 131). He criticizes Cartesian laws of motion for failing this test. The significance, then, of Leibniz's analysis of motion is not so much for the practice of physics, which should continue to consider motion as relative, but rather for metaphysics and reason itself. If physics is well grounded, if it ultimately makes sense, then it must be grounded in something real. Physics requires metaphysics for theoretical coherence. As Leibniz says in the *Discourse on Metaphysics*:

And it becomes more and more apparent that, although all the particular phenomena of nature can be explained mathematically or mechanically by those who understand them, nevertheless the general principles of corporeal nature and of mechanics itself are more metaphysical than geometrical, and belong to some indivisible forms or natures as the causes of appearances, rather than to corporeal mass or extension. This is a reflection capable of reconciling the mechanical philosophy of the moderns with the caution of some intelligent and well-intentioned persons who fear, with some reason, that we are withdrawing too far from immaterial beings, to the disadvantage of piety. (DM 18; AG 51–2)

Physics is not only reconcilable with a realm of immaterial substances; it requires them if motion is not to be simply illusory and incoherent. As with Leibniz's analysis of aggregates of extension, then, the move to metaphysics is both supported by physics and in turn explains the possibility of physics.

While physical phenomena can and must be accounted for through the laws of motion, the laws themselves depend on the existence of force as a real property of substances. This force must include a passive and active dimension. In one sense, active and passive forces are metaphysical, as fundamental properties of created substances. As such, Leibniz calls them 'primitive' forces. At the same time, these must explain actual force and resistance as it emerges in collision and interaction between bodies. Leibniz calls these 'derivative' forces. Physics uses only derivative forces, while metaphysics explains their origin in primitive forces. We can begin with the derivative forces, which have a direct role in explaining motion and collision. Leibniz defines force (taken as derivative active force) as the product of a body's mass and the square of its velocity. The significance of this conception of force lies in its relation to laws of collision. Descartes and his followers had argued that in any collision, the quantity of motion is conserved, taking quantity of motion as mass multiplied by velocity. In other words, if you calculate the quantity of motion in a number of bodies, that quantity will be the same before and after the collision, although the motion will be distributed differently among the various bodies. In fact, quantity of *motion* so defined (mass times speed) is not conserved in collisions. Rather, the quantity of *force* (mass times speed squared) is conserved. Leibniz gives several arguments for this, often in philosophical works like the *Discourse on Metaphysics* (DM 17–18; AG 49–52). He takes the fact that force, rather than motion, is conserved to show that matter must consist of more than extension and thus must involve something metaphysical (AG 173, 161–2). His point is that if matter consists only of extension, then the only relevant factors in a collision should be the amount of extension and its speed, in which case the quantity of motion should be conserved. In other words, if a moving body is nothing but extension changing place, then a body with one unit of mass and two units of velocity should be equivalent to a body with two units of mass and one unit of velocity. But this is not the case. The body with less mass and more speed does not equal the body with more mass and less speed. Thus matter must have some quality beyond extension that explains why the first body has more force than the second.

Leibniz uses derivative passive force to explain impenetrability and resistance to motion. To say that something is extended in space is to say that it maintains that space. That is, it resists intrusion into this space, it has some degree of impenetrability (AG 118). This focus on impenetrability as a fundamental quality of matter has deeper roots in Leibniz's conception of extension. We have seen that extension ultimately refers to an order of relations, the order of things that exist at the same time. Extension in itself is both phenomenal and incomplete – it presupposes something which is extended. Leibniz compares this to numbers:

[E]xtension is an abstraction from the extended thing, and it is no more a substance than number or multitude can be considered to be a substance; it represents only a certain non-successive ([unlike] duration) and simultaneous diffusion or repetition of a certain nature, or what comes to the same thing, it represents a multitude of things of the same nature, existing simultaneously, with a certain order among themselves. It is this nature, I say, that is said to be extended or diffused. And so the notion of extension is relative, that is, extension is the extension of something, just as we say that a multitude or duration is a multitude of something or the duration of something. (AG 179)

What is extended, then, is the quality of impenetrability. In regard to resistance, Leibniz argues that if matter is only extension in space, it should be indifferent to motion. It should move just as easily as it stays at rest, in which case a smaller moving body should easily move a larger body without any loss of motion. But this is not the case, which means that matter must have some intrinsic resistance to motion (DM 21; AG 53–4, 172–3, 123–4). This resistance, like impenetrability, must be rooted in something more than just extension across space. Both must be rooted in a passive force intrinsic to matter.

Derivative forces are determined through interaction with other bodies, through collision. As such, they are partly determined extrinsically – a body can have more or less derivative force depending on its situation. Nonetheless, because the laws determining these forces show that matter has an inherent lack of indifference toward motion, bodies themselves must have some intrinsic quality which explains these extrinsically determined derivative forces. Leibniz calls this inherent quality 'primitive force', active and passive. The reason why substances must have their own inherent forces follows more clearly from a claim that has been mentioned and will be discussed further in the next section: substances do not interact. Although the phenomenal world of physical things will still be analysed in terms of causal interaction, Leibniz argues that this interaction only determines the directions of internal force. He illustrates this in an argument in *A Species of Dynamics*. His argument relies on another of his key principles, which he calls the *principle of continuity*. According to this principle, there is no leap or gap in nature, all change happens gradually. In physics, this principle means there can be no immediate change or stop in motion. That is, when a moving body comes to rest, it must first slow down, passing through all speeds slower than its own until it reaches rest. Similarly, when a body changes direction, it must first gradually lose its current direction and then gradually gain speed in the other direction. Consequently, when two bodies collide and change directions, they must gradually lose their movement in one direction and then gradually acquire motion in the other direction. This kind of change cannot be explained by an exchange of something between the colliding bodies but must be explained by some innate force. As Leibniz describes it, when two bodies collide, they each compress. This compression gradually absorbs their forward motion, at the same time building up elastic force. When the forward motion stops, the bodies uncompress, which generates force in the opposite direction (AG 131–3). The details of this account do not matter here, but the key point is that the motion is based entirely on the force inherent in each body, which first cause the body to compress and then to rebound. No force is exchanged. This is the sense in which Leibniz says that derivative forces are modifications of internal primitive forces. Leibniz thus explains derivative force as: 'resulting from a limitation of primitive force through the collision of bodies with one another' (AG 119).

In describing the inherent active and passive force in a substance, Leibniz consciously reworks Aristotelian and Scholastic conceptions of substance. He argues that because matter alone cannot explain the unity or activity required for true being, we must rehabilitate the idea of form. Leibniz explicitly connects the primitive active force fundamental to all substances to Aristotle by calling it an *entelechy*, the basic act that constitutes a substance. He also calls it a substantial form. This primitive activity or striving in any substance grounds derivative force and the laws of motion in the material world. According to Leibniz, God is pure action, but all created, finite substances involve some passivity. Thus they all have primitive passive force, which explains not only resistance and impenetrability, but also the fact that finite substances are limited and suffer. Created substances both act and are acted upon; they are active and passive. This passive force is analogous to matter on the Aristotelian view and is expressed in the physical world as a body. Leibniz summarizes it:

> And so the resistance of matter contains two things, impenetrability or antitypy and resistance or inertia, and since they are everywhere equal in body or proportional to extension, it is in these things that I locate the nature of passive principle or matter. In just the same way I recognize a primitive entelechy in the active force exercising itself in various ways through motion and, in a word, something analogous to the soul, whose nature consists in a certain eternal law of the same series of changes, a series which it traverses unhindered. We cannot do without this active principle or ground of activity, for accidental or mutable active forces and motions themselves are certain modifications of a substantial thing, but forces and

actions cannot be modifications of a thing merely passive, such as matter is. Therefore, it follows that there is a first or substantial active thing modified by the added disposition of matter, or that which is passive. (AG 173)

Leibniz's use of Aristotelian concepts provides a perfect example of how he adapts concepts from the history of philosophy for his own purposes, and why this practice can be confusing. He believed Aristotle rightly recognized that there must be a principle of unity beyond what matter itself can provide and that this principle of unity is fundamental to what constitutes a substance. Similarly, Aristotle rightly recognized that both activity and passivity must be fundamental to the basic constituents of reality. These points were missing in the mechanistic view that took the physical world to consist of nothing but extension. Nonetheless, Leibniz places these Aristotelian insights into a fully modern context, radically shifting their meaning. For Leibniz, substances are thinking things, minds very much on the Cartesian model. Although they have inherent active and passive force, they are immaterial. Thus they can involve neither matter nor shape. Matter is only phenomenal. Even in accounting for the material world as a well-grounded phenomenon, Leibniz is far from an Aristotelian perspective. We have already seen how in his correspondence with Arnauld, he argues against coherent function as a principle of true unity in the material world. He rejects any appeal to substance or form in physics, which must provide explanations only in terms of collision and laws of motion.

III. SUBSTANCES AS POINTS OF VIEW ON THE UNIVERSE

We have now seen two of the basic characteristics Leibniz attributes to monads – unity and force. From the unity of these substances, it follows that they must be immaterial and that the material world must be a phenomenon grounded in them. What remains missing from this account of monads is the source of their diversity. There must be something within these substances to explain the actual diversity of the world, something that allows us to distinguish one substance from another. Leibniz calls his substances 'immaterial atoms', but they differ from atoms not only in being immaterial but also in their variety. Atoms were taken either to be completely uniform or to consist of a few basic types. Leibniz argued that this theory of uniform atoms fails to account for either the diversity of the universe or the differences between substances. Absolutely uniform atoms could never generate the qualitative differences actually experienced in the world. His argument that atoms do not sufficiently differ relies primarily on another of his basic principles, what he calls the *identity of indiscernibles*. Each substance must differ: 'For there are never two beings in nature that are perfectly alike, two beings in which it is not possible to discover an internal difference, that is, one founded on an intrinsic denomination' (M 9; AG 214). This principle derives primarily from the principle of sufficient reason. If two things are absolutely identical, there can be no reason to treat them differently. Thus there can be no reason why one is found here and another found there, and no way to explain any relationships or order among them (AG 333). This principle also follows from the concept-containment theory of truth, which claims that even seemingly extrinsic relations such as those in space must have some grounding in the substance itself, requiring that external differences express internal differences. Finally, the identity of indiscernibles is supported by this being the best possible world, taking best as maximizing variety and order. This world would clearly have much less variety if it were composed of uniform substances or even from a few basic types of substance. Leibniz uses this principle of the identity of indiscernibles to criticize material atoms: they cannot exist because they would be identical. The identity of indiscernibles thus requires that every immaterial atom or monad be unique and different from all the others. Under this requirement, the diversity of substances can only come about if substances contain a multiplicity of properties. This requirement for multiplicity is further supported by the fact that substances do not interact, so that the variety in our experience not only requires variety in the universe but also requires that this variety be contained in each substance.

The need for multiplicity in each substance seems to push Leibniz into a contradiction – on one side he must claim that substances are true unities and thus simple, while on the other side he must claim that substances contain an immense variety of properties. Insofar as a substance has diversity, how can it be truly one? A long passage from the *Principles of Nature and Grace, Based on*

Reason will serve both to summarize what we have established so far and to raise his solution to this problem:

> A *substance* is a being capable of action. It is simple or composite. A *simple substance* is that which has no parts. A *composite substance* is a collection of simple substances, or *monads*. *Monas* is a Greek word signifying unity, or what is one. Composites or bodies are multitudes; and simple substances – lives, souls, minds – are unities. There must be simple substances everywhere, because, without simples, there would be no composites. As a result, all of nature is full of life. Since the monads have no parts, they can neither be formed nor destroyed. They can neither begin nor end naturally, and consequently they last as long as the universe, which will be changed but not destroyed. They cannot have shapes, otherwise they would have parts. As a result, a monad, in itself and at a moment, can be distinguished from another only by its internal qualities and actions, which can be nothing but its *perceptions* (that is, the representation of the composite, or what is external, in the simple), or its *appetitions* (that is, its tendency to go from one perception to another) which are the principles of change. For the simplicity of a substance does not prevent a multiplicity of modifications, which must be found together in this same simple substance. (PNG 1–2; AG 207)

A substance must have a diversity which is not a diversity of parts or shapes, a diversity that does not conflict with unity and simplicity. The model Leibniz draws on to explain how such diversity and unity is possible is one quite close to us – our own consciousness. As I look out on this coffee shop, it is undeniable that I have a multiplicity of perceptions. I see tables and chairs, the chequered tiles on the floor, a handful of people, cars passing outside the window. In fact, one could say that this one view contains an infinite multiplicity of perceptions, a fact illustrated by the simple question, how many colours am I now seeing? One wooden chair contains an infinite variety of shades of brown. I could never fully describe what I see in any one of these people. I probably could not even fully describe the shades of colour on one strand of their hair. The infinite complexity of these perceptions is rooted in the infinite divisibility of any continuum – any aspect I pick out can be divided and divided into finer and finer detail. At the same time, it is just as undeniable that my perception has a kind of unity. My very ability to see *a* chair shows that I take all those shades of brown together as one. On a broader level, the whole view of the coffee shop seems to be distinctly *mine*. All these perceptions appear as a multiplicity in my one consciousness. This unity applies not only at any given moment but also over time. The multiplicity of qualities in my consciousness can change radically in a moment. I can simply turn my head, or close my eyes and picture myself lying in the sun on the beach, seeing as much detail as my imagination allows. Yet in spite of the radical shift from coffee shop to beach, it still seems to be my consciousness. These perceptions have a fundamental unity simply because they all are *mine*.

For Leibniz, consciousness not only provides the model for substance but gives us the idea of substance in the first place (AG 285–9). If I were aware only of my experience of the physical world, I would only experience infinitely divisible aggregates and I would never even come to the concept of a true substance. The idea of substance can only derive from reflection on my own consciousness, because that is my only experience of true unity. This basic claim that minds have unity was commonly accepted in the time of Leibniz. Descartes used this difference to argue for the radical distinction between mind and body. Taking substances as fundamentally mind-like also provides a way of understanding the force inherent in each substance. According to Leibniz, the multiplicity of consciousness always involves some tendency to change, some striving or desire. That could be the vague desire that leads me to turn my head and look out of the window without really thinking about it, thus changing my perceptions, or a more explicit desire to get up and get more coffee or go out of the door and walk home. Some of this inherent striving can also be seen as negative or resistant, as I might try to block out a conversation at a nearby table. Leibniz broadly calls this striving appetition, as we saw in the above quotation. Appetites are an internal, spontaneous force inherent in substances. Leibniz summarizes his view of substances as mind-like: 'we must say that there is nothing in things but simple substances, and in them, perceptions and appetite' (AG 181). The three elements Leibniz takes as essential to substance – unity,

force, and multiplicity – are all illustrated by the nature of consciousness itself.

The next step is to explain the specific content of these mind-
like monads. Leibniz says that each monad contains or expresses
the entire universe:

> [E]very substance is like a complete world and like a mirror of
> God or of the whole universe, which each one expresses in its
> own way, somewhat as the same city is variously represented
> depending upon the different positions from which it is viewed.
> Thus the universe is in some way multiplied by as many
> entirely different representations of his [God's] work. It can
> even be said that every substance bears in some way the char-
> acter of God's infinite wisdom and omnipotence and imitates
> him as much as it is capable. For it expresses, however confu-
> sedly, everything that happens in the universe, whether past,
> present, or future – this has some resemblance to an infinite
> perception or knowledge. And since all other substances in
> turn express this substance and accommodate themselves to it,
> one can say that it extends its power over all the others, in imi-
> tation of the creator's omnipotence. (DM 9; AG 42)

This passage from the *Discourse on Metaphysics* brings together
all of the main aspects of the content of each monad. We can
begin with the claim that each monad involves the infinity of the
entire universe. The primary support for this claim comes from
the concept-containment theory of truth. We have already seen
that the complete understanding of any one thing requires an
understanding of the causes or sufficient reasons for all the parti-
cularities of that thing, and that this sufficient reason ultimately
involves the entire universe. We have also seen that the concept of
substance was traditionally give two roles, one as a basis for individuation and the other as a subject of predicates. Leibniz
approaches substance by considering both of these roles. In
defining what is required of substance as a basis for individuation,
Leibniz argues that a substance must be a true unity, have force,
be immaterial, and have a multiplicity of perceptions. Leibniz
gives a different definition of substance from the perspective of
subject. Aristotle had defined a substance as something which can
be a subject of predicates but cannot itself be a predicate. So, for

example, green can be a subject of predicates, as we can speak of a vivid green, but it can also be a predicate, as we can call the table green. The table, in contrast, cannot itself be predicated of another thing. So the table is a substance; green is not. Leibniz says that this definition describes a property of substances but not their essence. He defines substance: '[W]e can say that the nature of an individual substance or of a complete being is to have a notion so complete that it is sufficient to contain and to allow us to deduce from it all the predicates of the subject to which this notion is attributed' (DM 8; AG 41). Leibniz's definition distinguishes substances both from modes and from abstract entities. We have already seen that the mind of God contains not only the ideas of particular things but also ideas of abstract things, like a triangle or justice. These 'things' differ from substances by the nature of their predicates. An abstract thing has a finite number of predicates, all of which can be established from the principle of non-contradiction. A substance involves an infinite number of predicates, giving it an exact place in a particular world. Thus the predicates of any substance involve the entire world, and since predicates are always contained in their subject, the entire universe must in some sense be contained in every substance. We can approach the same conclusion from the interconnection of all things. Anything in the universe has some relation to everything else. Although the universe is composed of discrete, separate substances, their mutual relatedness is expressed by the fact that the physical world grounded in them is a continuum, in which a change in one place has repercussions throughout the entire continuum. Leibniz describes this:

> And since everything is connected because of the plenitude of the world, and since each body acts on every other body, more or less, in proportion to distance, and is itself affected by the other through reaction, it follows that each monad is a living mirror, or a mirror endowed with internal action, which represents the universe from its own point of view and is ordered as the universe itself. (PNG 3; AG 207)

Because of the mutual influence of all things, the perceptions of which I am aware cannot be separated from the rest of the universe. This relatedness just expresses the fact that the concept of any one thing involves the concepts of all other things. A final strand of support follows from this being the best possible world, maximizing order and diversity or unity and variety. What could be more perfect than a world made up of monads that bring a perfect unity to a multiplicity as infinite and varied as the universe itself?

Having each monad contain the entire universe certainly increases the variety in each substance, but it seems to undermine diversity in the whole universe. That is, if all monads express the entire universe, aren't they all identical? Leibniz places variety between substances in two sources. The first is the degree of distinctness or clarity in the expression. Although all substances express the entire universe, only God can grasp the whole universe clearly. Human beings are relatively high on the scale of perfection, but what we can recognize and be aware of is constrained to a fairly narrow horizon. The perceptions of animals or things we would normally take as inanimate are even more confused and limited. Thus although each monad contains the entire universe, the amount *clearly* perceived varies by the amount of perfection in the substance. We have seen that Leibniz justifies metaphysical evil, that is, limitations in perfection, as necessary for the diversity of the whole universe. This metaphysical evil or limitation does not limit how much of the universe is contained in each monad but limits how much of the universe a monad clearly grasps or expresses. This account of limitation fits moral evil as well. Human beings do immoral things because they lack clear understanding; too much of the detail of the universe is beyond their distinct grasp. Leibniz's claim that each mind contains and in a sense perceives the entire universe may seem strange, but it is not so difficult to imagine. Imagine looking out over a vast landscape. The things around you are clearly perceived and recognized as distinct, but the further you look out, the more confused your perception becomes. A tree close by might be a trunk, branches and leaves; further out it is simply a tree; further still and there are only patches of trees, and then only blurs of darker green. At some point, things become completely confused and indistinct, reaching the limits of the horizon. What makes Leibniz's model stranger is that while we draw an absolute line at the horizon between what we perceive and what we do not, Leibniz projects a continuum of awareness, where what is beyond the horizon still reaches us, but at a level of vagueness that does not come into conscious awareness. This point will become clearer when we consider his doctrine of 'minute perceptions' in the following chapter.

If monads vary in how much of the universe they distinctly perceive, then a second source of diversity opens up. Monads can vary not only by how much they perceive but by which particular part of the universe they perceive more clearly. That is, as human beings, we express roughly the same amount of the universe, but I clearly express this coffee shop while you clearly express something quite different. Thus variety comes firstly through infinite degrees of perfection across different kinds of substances, and secondly from an infinite variation within each degree of perfection based on which part of the universe is more clear. Leibniz discusses this variation in terms of point of view, as we have seen in several passages. He explains in more detail in the *Monadology*:

> Just as the same city viewed from different directions appears entirely different and, as it were, multiplied perspectively, in just the same way it happens that, because of the infinite multitude of simple substances, there are, as it were, just as many different universes, which are, nevertheless, only perspectives on a single one, corresponding to the different points of view of each monad. (M 57; AG 220)

In another passage, Leibniz imagines God contemplating the idea of the best possible world, turning it and creating substances corresponding to each possible perspective (DM 14; AG 47). This difference between monads of similar levels of perfection can also be approached from the concept-containment theory of truth. While the complete concept of anything in the world contains the whole world as the sufficient reason for its existence, the orders in which those reasons unfold differ.

If unitary substances are the basic constituents of reality and these substances are immaterial beings that consist in a unity of perceptions, then anything that truly exists must exist as something like a mind. Where does that leave rocks, bushes, and tables? Arnauld poses this objection in his correspondence with Leibniz, arguing that if Leibniz's principles are true, then only human beings are real. At first, Leibniz answers with some hesitance. He responds that animals also have minds, a point denied by Descartes but on which Leibniz says common people all agree. He then says he does not dare to place limits on God by claiming that plants do not have minds (AG 82). Later, Leibniz confidently embraces what appears to be his only alternative:

> From this we can see that there is a world of creatures, of living beings, of animals, of entelechies, of souls in the least part of matter. Every portion of matter can be conceived as a garden full of plants, and as a pond full of fish. But each branch of a plant, each limb of an animal, each drop of its humors, is still another such garden or pond. And although the earth and air lying between garden plants, or the water lying between the fish of the pond, are neither plant nor fish, they contain yet more of them, though of a subtleness imperceptible to us, most often. (M 66–8; AG 222)

While this claim was strange, it was not unique to Leibniz. Spinoza, for example, had argued that all things are animate and have something like a mental existence along with their bodily existence.[3] To some degree, Leibniz was forced to this position by his theory of substance, but he supports it in two further ways. First, in a nice example of how he uses other sciences to support his philosophy, he appeals to the recent discoveries made by Anton van Leeuwenhoek and John Swammerdam using microscopes (WF 133). They had discovered microscopic organisms in seemingly dead things, like a drop of water. Leibniz took these discoveries as strong evidence that nothing is dead and that such microscopic organisms would be discovered in everything. The second argument again goes back to his claim that this is the best possible world. Surely a God maximizing order and diversity would create as many minds as possible, at all levels of consciousness: 'Thus there is nothing fallow, sterile, or dead in the universe...' (M 69; AG 222). As with many of Leibniz's claims, the omnipresence of life both receives support from God's goodness and in turn supports the claim that the world is richer and more perfect than it first appears. Leibniz is of course not claiming that all substances *think*. The monads of a tree or a rock exist as utterly confused, in a state much like we experience in a very deep sleep.

We can now summarize Leibniz's view of substance. Every substance exists as something like a mind, composed of perceptions and internal forces which cause those perceptions to vary over time. This perception always involves the entire universe, although only a small part of that universe comes within the horizon of conscious attention. Change, then, is always a process of some aspects of the universe becoming clearer while other aspects settle vaguely into the background. This change comes only from the internal striving of each substance, which causes its universe to unfold in different ways. Leibniz clarifies this spontaneous striving and unfolding in a series of replies to objections raised by Pierre Bayle. The core of Bayle's objections is the claim that even if a substance is a source of activity, it cannot cause complex changes in itself. He relies on a principle from physics – a body in motion will continue to move in a uniform line unless its course is changed by another body. So an atom may be able to maintain its own motion but cannot change the direction of that motion. He adds that a complex machine may cause complex motions in itself, but only through the interaction of the motions of its separate parts. Since a unitary substance lacks parts, it can only maintain its current state until altered by something outside of it.[4] Leibniz's response shows the intimate connection between the complexity of a monad's perceptions and the tendency of that monad to change. In explaining why atoms move uniformly while monads follow a complex law of change, Leibniz writes,

> It is because the atom (as we are imagining it, for there is no such thing in nature), even though it has parts, has nothing to cause any variety in its tendency, because we are supposing that these parts do not change their relations; on the other hand, the soul, though completely indivisible, involves a compound tendency, that is to say a multitude of present thoughts, each of which tends towards a particular change, depending on what is involved in it, and which are all in it at the same time, in virtue of the essential relatedness to all the other things in the world. (WF 249)

Material atoms are both too complex and too simple, which is why they cannot be the basic constituents of the world. They are too complex because they are always divisible into parts, but too simple because they cannot express their relation to the rest of the world. Their simplicity means that they can only retain and reproduce the current moment of their motion. Such uniform atoms cannot even maintain circular motion. Leibniz says that they are 'too stupid and imperfect': 'Matter remembers only what happened in the previous moment ... It remembers, that is to say, the direction of the tangent, but has no ability to remember the rule it would need to be given for diverging from that tangent and staying on the circumference' (WF 235). In contrast, the infinite complexity of a monad allows it to follow a complex law of change. This complexity makes a monad more like the complex machine which Bayle admits can cause changes in its own direction. Thus Leibniz sometimes calls monads 'immaterial automatons', basically, immaterial robots. If monads are comparable to any material thing, it would be the world itself, which develops in complex ways because of the relationships between the tendencies of all its parts. All of that complexity is expressed in each monad. Just as the real complexity of the universe allows it to change in complex ways without external interference, the real complexity of the representation of the universe in each monad allows it to change in complex ways on its own. In describing how a dog's soul might spontaneously change from feeling pleasure to feeling pain, Leibniz explains:

> The representation of the present state of the universe in the dog's soul produces in it the representation of the subsequent state of the same universe, just as in the things represented the preceding state actually produces the subsequent state of the world. *In a soul, the representations of causes are the causes of the representations of effects.* (WF 200)

The complex law of change in a monad means that the content of any monad extends beyond the present. Its present state expresses and arises from the complex tendencies of its past, and the tendencies in this present state express and determine its future. As Leibniz famously says: 'It has its present thoughts, from which the subsequent ones are born; and one can say that in the soul, as everywhere else, the present is big with the future' (WF 250).

IV. INTERACTION AND PRE-ESTABLISHED HARMONY

With Leibniz's conception of substance examined, we can now approach his claim that substances do not interact. The fact that each substance contains the entire universe and its principle of change explains why substances do not *need* to interact. Everything they need – the entire universe – is already contained in them. In fact, Leibniz takes the concept-containment theory of truth not only as showing that substances do not need to interact but as proving that they do not interact. Leibniz frequently moves from the claim that the concept of a substance must include the concepts of everything that will ever happen to it to the claim that a substance itself must include everything that will ever happen to it. Separating the two would make the concept false. That is, if something new came into a substance, then either something new would have to enter the concept of the substance, meaning the concept was not originally complete, or else, if the concept did not change, then the concept would have to have been false before or false now. More directly, if the concept of a substance is self-sufficient and true, then the substance itself must also be self-sufficient.

Leibniz's main arguments follow from the impossibility of interaction between substances. These arguments make the most sense in the context of discussions around the interaction of mind and body. Descartes had argued that minds and bodies were fundamentally different kinds of substances and, although mind/body dualism has been criticized, his analysis still has a basic plausibility. Consider a feeling of pain and the simultaneous collision of a toe and a wall. Clearly these have some relationship, but they seem radically different. The changes in bodies come only from movement in space, but a piercing feeling of pain cannot be understood in terms of either space or movement. Similarly, the perception of green seems radically different from the reflection of light across space. While Descartes allowed for interaction between minds and bodies in spite of their difference, many of those immediately after him denied the possibility of such interaction. Causality in the physical world was conceived as the collision of matter according to the general laws of motion. Thus bodies only cause effects insofar as they can cause something else to move, but how can they 'move' something that does not exist in space at all? Even if the collision of toe and wall starts a chain of movement leading into the brain, how can that movement eventually cause changes in an immaterial mind? How can it cause a feeling of pain? Leibniz, like most of his contemporaries, concluded that it cannot, and that the interaction of mind and body is impossible. If we set aside interaction between minds and bodies, though, what kind of interaction remains possible? The only remaining form of interaction for a mind would be directly with other minds, something like mind reading or ESP. Such interaction is even more difficult to conceive of and something few claim to experience. Thus Leibniz's claim that no substances interact is only a small, reasonable step from the more widely accepted claim that mind and body do not interact.

On a general level, the claim that substances do not interact follows from the very idea of substance. In order to consider a substance as one thing, it must have independence from other things. Insofar as it interacts and depends on other substances, it lacks this independence. Leibniz's specific argument focuses on the necessary unity of a substance, which entails that substances have no parts. To say that two things inter-act is to say that something from one enters into and changes the other. Otherwise, we could only say that one substance changed just before the second one, not that the first substance caused a change in the second. A few basic problems follow. As a unity, one substance cannot have parts that it can break off and give to another, just as it cannot receive and incorporate new parts. The point of Leibniz's famous claim that monads have no windows is not so much that we cannot look out of the window on to something else, although, indeed, we cannot, but rather than there are no windows that we can open in order to pass parts in or out. Thus he sometimes also says that monads lack doors (DM 26; AG 58). Furthermore, what would be the status of these parts that are exchanged? Any quality that could detach from one substance, move, and attach itself to another substance would require its own independent being. For at least a moment, it would not be a mode of the first substance or a mode of the second substance. In order to be independent, the quality so exchanged would have to become a substance itself, which would mean that first one substance splits into two and then two substances merge into one, all of which would contradict the idea of a substance not being divisible into or composed of parts. Leibniz sees any view of interaction as involving absurd qualities, which he says are thought to fly in and out of substances like pigeons (NE 379). Ultimately, our conception of interaction is not as clear as it might seem. It derives from observation of changes in material phenomena, changes consisting in the rearrangement of matter in space. This rearrangement appears as interaction because we confuse aggregates with unitary things and then say those things interact, but all this interaction really amounts to is the entering and exiting of parts in and out of patterns of aggregation. One part displaces another, but never somehow reaches inside of another and causes it to change. Leibniz brings together the different strands of this argument in the *Monadology*:

> There is also no way in which it could make sense for a monad to be altered or changed internally by any other created thing. Because there is nothing to rearrange within a monad, and there is no conceivable internal motion in it which could be excited, directed, increased, or diminished, in the way that it can in a composite, where there is change among the parts. Monads have no windows, through which anything could come in or go out. And accidents [i.e. qualities] cannot detach themselves and stroll about outside of substances, as the Scholastics' sensible species used to; so neither substance nor accident can come into a monad from outside. (M 7; AG 268)

Leibniz provides a strong argument that if we commit ourselves to an ontology based on unitary substances, then we must accept that those substances do not interact. He also makes a strong case that for things to have any reality at all, they must be rooted in unitary substances. Nonetheless, his arguments seem to defy common sense. The plausibility of his account only becomes clear if we follow him in taking substances not as physical aggregates like a cup or human body but rather as unitary consciousnesses. From this perspective, Leibniz appears as an astute observer of consciousness, giving an account significantly more plausible than our commonsense views of interaction. Consciousness seems to have an irreducible element of what we might call 'mine-ness'. I do not experience things as independent and objectively existing; insofar as they exist in my consciousness, insofar as I am aware of them at all, things exist in relation to my own point of view. In consciousness, things exist as my representations of them. I see you across a room. Do you as you are in yourself enter my consciousness? No. I see you from a certain perspective, which is why my perceptions change as I walk around you even though you yourself do not change. In this sense, whatever exists in this unitary consciousness that is my monad always exists in a certain perspective. I might vary my perspective and fight against my biases, but this process only yields more accurate representations, for the very reason that they always remain part of my unitary consciousness. I never step out of my mind to get to the thing itself. This is exactly what Leibniz means when he says that each monad exists as a certain perspective on the world. When we talk about someone having a 'world-view' or say that they are 'in their own world' we come close to Leibniz's meaning.

Even if we agree that all we ever know are representations of the world based on our particular point of view, we might still want to say that these representations are caused by the things themselves. The first problem would be to explain how a material thing can have any causal effect on something like a consciousness. Setting that problem aside, do we experience this kind of interaction? Does a hole in consciousness rip open and something new fly in like a pigeon? Not at all. Leibniz seems right in saying that consciousness does not have windows or doors through which things pass. Instead, things fade into a background or emerge from a vague horizon. New experiences never appear as discrete parts leaping in, but unfold as part of a context or point of view, which is exactly how Leibniz describes experience. Even causation within consciousness fits Leibniz's description. Let's say you walk over and kick me in the shin. How would I experience this? In my perspectival view, certain perceptions of you get larger as you come closer. I look down and see your foot move and collide with my shin. Pain arises. We might imagine that some foot exists outside my possible experience and then somehow through motion mysteriously injects pain into my consciousness, perhaps tossing it in through an open window, but in that case we are denying our experience for the sake of our own metaphysical assumptions. I experience a series of representations causing other representations – an image of you coming closer, moving in a certain way, then followed by a feeling of pain. We have seen Leibniz give just this kind of description in accounting for how a dog experiences a shift from pleasure to pain: 'the representations of causes are the causes of the representations of effects' (WF 200).

Finally, we might accept all of this as an accurate description of what it is like to be a consciousness, but still say that there is something like interaction happening not between minds but within consciousness itself. Leibniz would not disagree. While he denies that *substances* can interact, he does not deny all interaction. His point is that interaction must be conceived within the unfolding of one consciousness rather than through interaction between different consciousnesses. The entire universe exists within each monad. We could say that everything in the universe is expressed as modes within each monad; as modes within one substance, they can interact. Leibniz's position in a way resembles that of Spinoza. Like Spinoza, Leibniz argues that interaction between substances is incomprehensible, and that any possible interaction must take place between the modes of one substance. While Spinoza concludes that there is only one substance, Leibniz concludes that there is an infinite number of substances, each unfolding from a different point of view.

The final element in Leibniz's basic view of the world is the relationship between these fundamentally independent monads. Leibniz claims that God could have made a universe in which each monad had a completely separate world following its own path without regard to any other, but such a world would run against God's goodness (WF 204). The diversity of monads must combine with some principle of order. Leibniz accounts for this order through one of his most famous terms, *pre-established harmony*. Although pre-established harmony explains the relationships between all substances, Leibniz focuses on the relationship between mind and body, which was one of the central problems in early modern thought. Leibniz considers two possible solutions, aside from his own. The first is that mind and body directly interact. We have already seen the main reason Leibniz and most of his contemporaries rejected this position – bodies can only cause effects through motion and collision and so have no way of influencing an immaterial consciousness. The second solution is known as 'Occasionalism', and was associated primarily with Nicolas Malebranche, one of the leading philosophers of the seventeenth century.[5] The Occasionalists accepted that there must be some influence between mind and body, but also held that direct causal interaction was impossible. The solution was to appeal to God, who made changes in bodies based on the actions of minds and in minds based on the actions of bodies. My mental choice to move my arm becomes the occasion on which God actually makes my physical arm move. This view was primarily accepted due to a lack of alternatives, but it was closely connected to a view of matter as fundamentally passive and incapable of generating or even sustaining motion on its own. Thus all motion in the physical world ultimately depends on God, who determines those motions while considering the intentions of minds. Although this view now seems implausible, Leibniz takes it more seriously than direct causal interaction. In his view, Occasionalism might be difficult to believe, but direct causal interaction was impossible.

Leibniz primarily criticized Occasionalism for relying too much on direct intervention from God. He called it a system full of miracles, a system that literally required a *Deus ex machina*. While God *could* perform such miracles, a system that continually relied on them falls short of God's goodness and power. Several of Leibniz's correspondents thought this charge of relying on miracles was unfair. The Occasionalists did not imagine God running back and forth, adjusting things as if moving chess pieces. The action of God on matter was regular and consistent, and thus not really miraculous. Leibniz's response reveals his conception of miracles but also his commitment to scientific explanation:

Let us see, however, whether the system of occasional causes really doesn't involve a perpetual miracle. Here it is said that it does not, because the system holds that God acts only according to general laws. I agree that he does, but in my view that isn't enough to remove miracles. Even if God produced them all the time, they would still be miracles, if the word is understood not in the popular sense, as a rare and marvellous thing, but philosophically, as something that exceeds the power of created things. It isn't sufficient to say that God has made a general law, for in addition to the decree there has also to be some natural way of carrying it out. It is necessary, that is, that what happens should be explicable in terms of the God-given nature of things. Natural laws are not as arbitrary and groundless as many think. (WF 205)

Leibniz applies this same interpretation of miracles to several other cases, for example, arguing against Locke's claim that bodies might be able to think and to Newton's claim that bodies have an attractive force. Leibniz's underlying point is that changes in the physical world must be explicable by the nature of the physical world. Although God could violate that nature and enact miracles, to do so regularly would be inefficient and unworthy of God's perfection. While the discussion centres on the question of miracles, the real issue is the need for coherence in scientific explanations.

Occasionalism runs into a deeper problem in allowing any influence, even indirect, between minds and bodies. The problem with the interaction of mind and body goes beyond the fact that minds do not exist in space. According to the new science, motion in bodies is entirely explained by the collisions of matter according to general laws of motion. Every physical event should be entirely explained or determined by other physical causes. One consequence of this view must be some principle of conservation, that new force cannot just enter a system from nowhere. Causality in minds, however, seems quite different. Some claimed that the choices of minds were free in the sense of undetermined. Others, like Leibniz, claimed that the choices of minds were causally determined, but that they were determined by deliberation and reason. Part of the drive behind the split between mind and body throughout this era was the commitment to a mechanistic account of causality in bodies along with a reluctance to apply this kind of blind causality to the determination of minds. This split conflicted with the general desire for a unified science; it was just distasteful to admit two radically distinct accounts of causality, one for bodies and one for minds. The real problem, though, comes with interaction between these two realms. Insofar as mind has any influence on body, it must disrupt the laws of motion. Suddenly a body begins to move, based on a choice of the mind rather than the collision of matter. The laws of conservation are violated, and any account of the physical world solely through physics becomes impossible. Physics would have to account constantly for the causality of minds, a causality inexplicable in physical terms. Descartes tried to avoid this problem by arguing that minds cannot create new motion in bodies but can change the direction of that motion. This solution was rejected, though, when it was determined that direction of motion also must be conserved in physical interactions. This problem is more clear in the case of direct causal interaction, but it applies to any attempt to give mind influence over body, and Leibniz saw it as applying to Occasionalism as well (T 156–7). Aside from abandoning physics, there seem to be only two possible responses to this problem. One could abandon dualism, which in this context would mean claiming either that only bodies exist (materialism) or that only minds exist (idealism), or one could view mind and body as acting in a parallel or coordinated way, each according to its own laws but without any mutual influence, as Spinoza does.

Leibniz's conception of substance places him in a perfect position to address these difficulties. The need for influence between substances followed mostly from what seemed like a commonsense view, that there is some coordination between events in our bodies and events in our minds. This *coordination*, though, does not prove *influence*. Moreover, this coordination itself is suspect – if all we know is what appears in our consciousness, how do we really know that there is a physical world outside us that corresponds to our experience? We could, after all, be dreaming, or, as Leibniz says, it could be that only God and myself exist. The main argument for influence was that some changes in bodies and in minds seem to be only explicable through their interaction. Pierre Bayle pushes this argument from both directions (WF 225–32). Bodies sometimes act with a complexity that seems to defy physical explanation. Consider the building of a cathedral. Can it really be explained without reference to the minds of the architects and engineers? The body of the architect would have to be an extremely sophisticated machine capable of generating building plans, which are then carried out by other highly sophisticated body-machines. With advances in computer technology and in studies of the brain, such a story now seems quite plausible, but it did not seem so to Leibniz's contemporaries. Leibniz simply argues that human beings already can create complex machines and that one cannot infer the absolute limits of physical machines from the limits of current technology, particularly if the author of these bodily machines is omnipotent and omniscient. Conversely, it was argued that some changes in our mind can only be explained by the influence of our body – why else would a tear in my skin be followed by a feeling of pain in my mind? We have already seen Leibniz's reply to this argument as made by Bayle. Each substance dynamically unfolds an infinitely complex expression of the universe. This complexity explains all of its changes, including that shift from pleasure to pain. Thus Leibniz claims that entirely separate accounts can be given of mind and body, reconciling materialism and idealism:

> So pure materialists, like the Democriteans, and also formalists, like the Platonists and the Peripatetics, are partly right and partly wrong. The Democriteans had the perfectly justified belief that human as well as animal bodies are automata and do everything completely mechanically; but they were wrong to believe that these machines are not associated with an immaterial substance or form, and also that matter could think. The Platonists and Peripatetics believed that the bodies of animals and men are animated, but they were wrong to think that souls change the rules of bodily movement; in this way they took away the automatic side of animal and human bodies. The Cartesians were right to reject the influence, but went wrong in taking away the automatic side of man and the thinking side of animals. I think we should keep both sides for both things: we should be Democritean and make all actions of bodies mechanical and independent of souls, and we should also be more than Platonic and hold that all actions of souls are immaterial and independent of mechanism. (WF 234–5).

We see here again how Leibniz's metaphysical concerns serve to establish the material world as the realm of physics, something threatened if we fail to keep the realm of minds separate from the phenomenal world of bodies.

Since Leibniz has already argued that each substance develops independently according to its own law of change, all that is required for coordination between substances is some coordination in these laws. With this, each substance will independently change in coordination with other changes in the universe, through a pre-established harmony. Leibniz illustrates this position and its two alternatives with the example of two clocks keeping exactly the same time (WF 192). In seeing these two clocks side by side, we might be perplexed at the harmony between them. To explain it, we might imagine that the movement in the first clock immediately causes the movement of the second clock. This explanation is that of interaction, which might be possible for clocks but is not possible between mind and body (or any true substances). Failing with interaction, we might imagine that as soon as the first clock moves, some hidden being sees it and manually makes the second clock move. This explanation is that of the Occasionalists. While it is possible, an outstanding inventor like God should come up with a more efficient design. The third possibility is to explain their harmony through the precision of their own machinery, expressing the skill of their makers. They maintain exactly the same movements not because of any influence between them but simply because they each independently keep precise time. This is Leibniz's explanation for the relationship between all substances, pre-established harmony.

Arnauld argues that Leibniz's account is no less miraculous than that of the Occasionalists, since it still relies on God to explain the coordination of individual substances (e.g. WF 119–23). Bayle also argues that this account is miraculous, because it requires more of a substance than can really be explained by its nature; every substance would have to keep track of changes in an infinity of other substances (WF 225–9). Leibniz's response to these charges follows from the fact that each monad expresses and unfolds the same universe. Action and expression are the very essence of a substance. To be a monad is just to be a unified, dynamic perspective. Thus the changes in any monad are entirely explicable through the nature of substance and require no action from God beyond the initial act of creation. The coordination between monads also follows efficiently. As we have seen, in a sense, every monad is identical in containing and unfolding the very same universe. They differ only by how much and which part of that one universe they express clearly: 'In fact when we say that each monad, soul, or mind has received a specific law, we must add that this is only a variation of the general law which orders the universe; it is like the way in which the same town appears different from the different points of view from which it is seen' (WF 239). Monads relate just as perspectives relate. When we witness the same event, we each have a slightly different experience. We see that event from different directions and we notice different things. Yet we can easily talk to each other about our experiences, and even learn more details through that discussion. This harmony and difference between our experiences requires no extraordinary explanation, no direct interaction between our minds or mysterious being adjusting our thoughts to each other. Our experiences are coordinated because they are each a point of view on the same thing. Leibniz's account must differ slightly from our usual understanding, because we do not interact with the universe but are rather created with this unfolding perspective from the beginning, but the coordination of minds is achieved in just the same way. This relationship between minds provides a perfect illustration of Leibniz's conception of perfection –

> The marvel is that the sovereign wisdom has found in representing substances a way to vary the same world at the same time to an infinite degree, for since the world already contains in itself an infinite variety, and has that variety diversely expressed by an infinity of different representations, it possesses an infinity of infinities, and could not be more appropriate to the nature and intentions of its inexpressible author, who exceeds in perfection everything that can be thought. (WF 239)

The best possible world consists of an infinity of mind-like simple substances. These substances do not interact but each one expresses all the others. Within each monad, this universe is experienced as existing in space and time. We have already seen that Leibniz takes space, time, matter, and motion all as well-grounded phenomena. That claim can now be more fully understood. The order of monads is experienced within each mind as a spatial and temporal continuum. Space and time are simply the ways we experience the relations between substances. They are subjective aspects of conscious experience, not things existing independently in the world. Nonetheless, they are well grounded, expressing the actual relationships between immaterial substances. Given the phenomenal status of space, time, and the physical world, and the fact that substances do not interact, causality cannot be fully real. The very possibility of science, though, requires causality to have some grounding in real things. To grasp Leibniz's account of causality, we must consider an example of causal interaction in the terms he has set up so far. We can return to the earlier example of you kicking me in the shin. That same event which I described as in my consciousness would also exist in your consciousness, but from a different point of view. Your vision of your foot and my shin would exist from a slightly different angle. More significantly, the whole event would be preceded in your consciousness by some other thoughts, perhaps the desire to give a memorable refutation of the claim that substances do not interact. The event in your consciousness would be followed by some sensation in your toes, but not the pain that appeared in my mind. If we talk only about the universe as it exists as a representation in my consciousness or your consciousness, then we have no problem in claiming that one representation, you, caused a change in another representation, me. That kind of interaction is really modal interaction within one substance, either your consciousness or mine. Strictly speaking, though, no substances interacted. Nonetheless, is there any relation between them that might be expressed as causation? That is, what would allow us to call causation well grounded? First, you can be said to cause the event because the reasons for the event are more clearly expressed in your mind. The reason for the event is contained in each of us, but you recognize it distinctly through the deliberation that led to your action. I am left merely to guess your intention. Thus this change that we both express is better explained through you than through me. In other words, although you do not cause the event, you do explain it. Second, this event takes place according to your wishes and against mine. I suffer the action, while you choose it. In this sense, I can be said to be passive in relation to the event, while you can be said to be active in relation to it. Finally, this event expresses a decrease in my perfection and an increase in yours, at the very least because it expresses my weakness and your strength. Leibniz summarizes these aspects of causality in the *Monadology*:

> The creature is said to *act* externally insofar as it is perfect, and *to be acted upon* by another insofar as it is imperfect. Thus we attribute *action* to a monad insofar as it has distinct perceptions, and *passion*, insofar as it has confused perceptions. And one creature is more perfect than another insofar as one finds in it that which provides an *a priori* reason for what happens in the other; and this is why we say it acts on the other. (M 49–50; AG 219)

None of these relations are causal in the usual sense, but they ground the phenomenon called causality. The connection between these relationships and causality is clearer in considering God's choice to create this particular world. To form a possible world, substances must be accommodated to each other so as to avoid contradictions. Thus changes in one substance require changes in other substances. More exactly, the choice to create a certain substance determines the creation of other substances. In some cases, creating a substance with a certain amount of perfection requires the creation of other substances with less perfection. The creation of the you that kicks me requires the creation of the me that is kicked. In this sense, we could say that the reason for the creation of the me that is kicked goes along with the reasons for creating the you that kicks. In this aspect, the choice involves accommodating me to you, and the reason for this lies more in you than in me. Leibniz uses several terms for this version of causality: an ideal cause (T 159), a final cause, a model cause (WF 116). He explains how we could even still speak of the mind and body interacting:

> For in so far as the soul has perfection and distinct thoughts, God has accommodated the body to the soul, and has arranged beforehand that the body is impelled to execute its orders. And in so far as the soul is imperfect and as its perceptions are confused, God has accommodated the soul to the body, in such sort that the soul is swayed by the passions arising out of corporeal representations. This produces the same effect and the same appearance as if the one depended immediately upon the other, and by the agency of a physical influence. (T 159)

This section makes clear the way Leibniz's tendency to speak on different levels can be confusing – his discussions of mind–body interaction or causality are in one sense true but in another sense false, depending on the context.

Leibniz frequently appeals to pre-established harmony in discussions of the relationship between mind and body, but strictly speaking, bodies are phenomena of a spatial continuum. All relationships are between different mind-like substances. What then ultimately is the relation between mind and body? The relation of mind and body brings together a number of points already examined. We normally take a body to be an aggregate of matter with a coordinated function. The parts of a body can be infinitely divided into smaller and smaller units. For a human being, blood flows in repeated patterns controlled by the heart, which in turn serves the body as a whole. Often, that body acts according to the decisions of the mind. As matter itself is a well-grounded phenomenon, a physical body must be an expression of mind-like monads. We should thus be able to shift from this description of the body as a phenomenon to the relations of real substances. Every portion of matter expresses an infinity of living substances. These substances vary in degrees of perfection or expressiveness and so can be grouped into hierarchies of perfection, which amount to hierarchies of explanation. At the top of that hierarchy is my mind, the monad which is my own consciousness and which I identify as 'I'. Below this are other monads, also mind-like but with much less expressive power, corresponding to the various organs, below which there are more, even less expressive monads, and so on to infinity:

> It is true that the number of simple substances that enter into a mass, however small, is infinite, since besides the soul, which brings about the real unity of the animal, the body of the sheep (for example) is actually subdivided – that is, it is again, an assemblage of invisible animals or plants which are in the same way composites, outside of that which also brings about their real unity. Although this goes on to infinity, it is evident that, in the end, everything reduces to these unities, the rest or the results being nothing but well-founded phenomena. (AG 147)

Monads at a higher level in this hierarchy generally 'cause' the changes in monads at lower levels, because those at the top are more perfect and thus more clearly express the reasons for these changes. We could also say that in creating this world, God chose the lower monads to accommodate the higher ones. This causal relationship, however, is not absolute. Although the mind is more perfect than the monads of the body, the mind is still very limited and some reasons are more clearly expressed in the body than in the mind. In those cases, the mind is said to be acted on by the body. The relationship between the monad which is my mind and those of my body is not different in kind from the relationship between my mind and any other substance. Nonetheless, the monads making up one person are much more frequently accommodated to each other and in this sense have more causal dependency. This closer relationship is expressed as the coordinated functioning of a material body. Insofar as we can call that body one, it is because all of those monads are accommodated to one monad, which can be considered the mind or form of that thing. Thus we see how substance comes back to play a role in individuation, and why Leibniz sometimes echoes Aristotle in calling the mind the 'form' of the body (WF 113).

The organization of monads into hierarchies of bodies grounds the further organization of monads according to point of view. Leibniz writes,

> Thus, although each created monad represents the whole universe, it more distinctly represents the body which is particularly affected by it, and whose entelechy it constitutes. And just as this body expresses the whole universe through the interconnection of all matter in the plenum, the soul also represents the whole universe by representing this body, which belongs to it in a particular way. (M 62; AG 221)

We experience the world from the point of view of our body, which is to say that the way we relate to the rest of the universe appears in our consciousnesses as the spatial relationship between our body and the rest of the world. What comes in and out of clarity in our consciousness corresponds to what comes closer and moves further from our body. On a more basic level, our perspective arises from our senses, which give information according to how other bodies impact them. This view of body draws together some of the points with which we began this chapter. Insofar as I have a perspective, that is, insofar as I clearly express only a limited part of the universe, I am imperfect and limited. Because of that limitation, changes can happen in my consciousness which are best explained by things outside of me. This imperfection is manifested as my having a body, which centres the limitations of my perspective and which acts on me and allows other things to act on me. My body renders me dependent on other things, for food, warmth, protection, and even for perception. In connecting embodiment and limitation, Leibniz reworks a long tradition of associating the body with passivity and imperfection. This connection leads him to claim that all created monads must have bodies. Since all monads have some imperfection, all monads have an embodied perspective on the world.

This embodiment persists even after death. Monads are naturally indestructible, going in and out of existence only by an act of God. This indestructibility follows from the very concept of a monad – since monads do not interact, they cannot create or destroy each other. Moreover, our usual conception of creation and destruction relates only to the composition and decomposition of parts, and thus cannot apply to true unities. Death, insofar as we know it, is not the annihilation of the body but rather the dis-integration of its parts. Similarly, things are not created out of nothing but rather by gathering and arranging materials that already exist. In either case, nothing is truly destroyed or created; rather, parts that continue in existence are rearranged. Creation and destruction in the radical sense of coming into and going out of existence is miraculous, done only by God. Consequently, the *destruction* of a monad or soul upon the death of the body would be miraculous; *immortality* is natural. Leibniz thus takes his system of monads as proving the immortality of the soul, one of the main concerns of natural theology. Leibniz complicates his position in two ways. Although his claim that our experience of creation and destruction only comes from the rearranging of parts is plausible, we still tend to think that the mind or soul of an animal appears at birth and disappears at death. On Leibniz's account, this creation and destruction would require perpetual miraculous action by God, something Leibniz generally refuses. This continual destruction of animal monads would also seem like a waste. A more efficient and perfect system would have those animal monads transform and become other things, so that the same material took on diverse forms. For these reasons, Leibniz moves from the claim that monads are not *naturally* created and destroyed to the claim that they are in fact eternal. All monads were created at the beginning of the world and all will exist as long as the world.

This position leads to the second complication – where are all these monads before their bodies are born, and what happens to them when their bodies die? Human souls go on to Heaven or Hell, but these are available only to rational beings that can be held accountable for their actions. The obvious solution would be reincarnation, but Leibniz rejects that. He may see reincarnation as a threat to the existence of Heaven or Hell, but his argument comes from the inseparability of a monad from its embodied perspective. As Leibniz puts it in response to Locke's discussion of identity – 'On my hypotheses souls are not 'indifferent to any parcel of matter', as it seems to you that they are; on the contrary they inherently express those portions with which they are and must be united in an orderly way' (NE 240). Switching bodies would require too radical and discontinuous a change in the monad itself. Thus the second complication in Leibniz's account of immortality is that, in a sense, the body of every monad is also immortal. The inseparability of a monad and its embodiment again shows how the relationship of expression between the physical world and the real world of monads gives more significance to the physical world than a more familiar picture that sees bodies as independently real. If mind and body are both independently real, then, no matter their connection, they remain different things that in principle can be separated. For Leibniz, mind and body cannot be separated precisely because body is just an expression of the mind's relation to the rest of the world. Consequently, death marks a *transformation* rather than *transmigration* from one body to another:

> Thus not only souls, but also animals cannot be generated and cannot perish. They are only unfolded, enfolded, reclothed, unclothed, and transformed; souls never entirely leave their body, and do not pass from one body into another that is entirely new to them. There is therefore no *metempsychosis*, but there is *metamorphosis*. Animals change, but they acquire and leave behind only parts. In nutrition this happens a little at a time and by small insensible particles, though continually, but it happens suddenly, visibly, but rarely, in conception or in death, which causes animals to acquire or lose a great deal all at once. (PNG 6; AG 209)

Basically, at death, the monad's body shrinks and simplifies. This may seem strange empirically, but Leibniz again drew support from recent developments in biology following the use of microscopes:

> Modern investigations have taught us, and reason confirms it, that living things whose organs are known to us, that is, plants and animals, do not come from putrefaction or chaos, as the ancients believed, but from preformed seeds, and consequently, from the transformation of preexistent living beings. (PNG 6; AG 209)

He specifically cites Leeuwenhoek and Swammerdam as holding his view of the generation of animals. Leibniz simply goes the next logical step to claim that a similar process happens at death – it is only natural that something which is generated by transformation will be destroyed in the same way. Leibniz also appeals to descriptions of near-death experiences – in both human beings and other animals – as showing that the boundary between life and death is not as radical as one might think (WF 133). As the above passage from the *Principles of Nature and Grace* suggests, death is just a more extreme form of the way we transform from moment to moment. This account of life and death draws further support from Leibniz's principle of continuity, that nature never acts through a leap (NE 58). To fully understand Leibniz's view of these transformations, we must recall that the body of an animal is an aggregate that expresses a hierarchy of other monads. Upon death, that aggregation and hierarchy disintegrates, but each monad continues to be expressed as some organic material. The monad that was dominant in the hierarchy, which we might call the mind of the animal, loses its relation to the other parts, a change which marks its own loss of power and perfection and a decline in the clarity of its perceptions. It becomes a much simpler monad, perhaps the kind of thing Leeuwenhoek found in his microscopes. It also becomes the kind of thing that might be incorporated into new hierarchies and arrangements, perhaps by being eaten by worms. Human beings, however, are not part of this process. Their unique qualities render them susceptible to the demands of justice, which requires that they maintain self-consciousness after death. To see why, we must examine how rational monads differ from the monads of rocks, trees, and dogs.

CHAPTER 4

RATIONAL MINDS

I. MINUTE PERCEPTIONS AND LEVELS OF AWARENESS

The preceding chapter showed how Leibniz radically changes the Cartesian conception of the relationship and status of mind and body. Rather than a world composed of two radically different kinds of things – extended substances and thinking substances – Leibniz argues for a world made up only of simple, mind-like substances, or monads. All created monads are expressed in other minds as bodies ordered in space and time. Body becomes a phenomenal expression of the immaterial substances that compose reality. One consequence of this reconfiguration of mind and body is a shift and weakening of the line between human beings and other animals. For Descartes, the uniqueness of human beings is quite clear. All things exist as bodies, determined by the collision of matter according to physical laws. Some of these things are quite complex, like dogs and trees, but all are determined by the blind laws of physics. Feeling and awareness have no place in this material world. Human beings are unique because in addition to a body, we have a soul or mind. Thus only human beings are capable of consciousness and feeling, even basic feelings like that of pain. This distinction between human beings and other animals is reinforced by immortality. As composites, bodies are destroyed by the decomposition of their parts; as unities, minds cannot be so destroyed. Minds are naturally immortal. Since only human beings have minds, only human beings are immortal. The restriction of minds to human beings allows human properties like reason and choice to be fundamental properties of any mind. In other words, for Descartes, to be a mind is to be rational, free and subject to divine justice.

This clear and radical distinction between human beings and other animals is not available to Leibniz. He explicitly conceives substance in general by analogy with the human mind. All substances, from rocks to dogs to human beings, have something like perceptions and appetites. Similarly, as true unities, all substances are naturally immortal. Rather than distinguish human beings by their having a mind, then, Leibniz must distinguish different kinds of minds, and thus different levels of consciousness. Human minds are distinguished from other monads in two ways. First, rational minds not only express the universe of monads, but also express the mind of God. This relationship to the ideas in the mind of God gives us access to necessary truths and allows for the possibility of self-consciousness, which only rational minds have. Second, human beings are distinguished by the greater clarity and distinctness of their perceptions. The monads of rocks have perceptions that are utterly confused and indistinguishable. Animals perceive things in a more focused way, while human perception is even more focused. The first difference is a radical one. Human beings have access to necessary truths; animals and rocks do not. The second difference is one of degree. Clarity of perceptions range across a continuum, with the confused perceptions of rocks near the bottom and human perceptions near the top. That hiearchy, though, is not absolute. In any moment of consciousness, many of our perceptions are extremely confused, and over time, we vary in the clarity of our perceptions, sometimes, as in a deep sleep, coming close to the mental being of rocks. The first distinction will be examined in the following section. This section will examine the second distinction, based on clarity and distinctness of perceptions.

Leibniz explains his position in the *Monadology*:

If we wish to call *soul* everything that has *perceptions* and *appetites* in the general sense I have just explained, then all simple substances or created monads can be called souls. But, since sensation is something more than a simple perception, I think that the general name of monad and entelechy is sufficient for simple substances which only have perceptions, and that we should only call those substances *souls* where perception is more distinct and accompanied by memory. (M 19; AG 215)

What distinguishes a feeling as more distinct than a mere perception is that a feeling involves recognition. One does not just experience a flow of perceptions but is able to pick out some of those perceptions and become aware of them. This attention requires memory, because it requires us to retain a perception long enough to note it. In the *Principles of Nature and Grace*, Leibniz makes the same distinction as one between perception and apperception: 'Thus it is good to distinguish between *perception*, which is the internal state of the monad representing external things, and *apperception*, which is *consciousness*, or the reflective knowledge of this internal state, something not given to all souls, nor at all times to a given soul' (PNG 4; AG 208). *Apperception* is one of Leibniz's key terms, referring to perceptions which are consciously recognized. All monads consist of perceptions and appetites, but that does not mean all monads are conscious. The kind of perception that a rock has is difficult to imagine, but Leibniz says we sometimes experience something similar:

> For we experience within ourselves a state in which we remember nothing and have no distinct perception; this is similar to when we faint, or when we are overwhelmed by a deep, dreamless sleep. In this state the soul does not differ sensibly from a simple monad; but since this state does not last, and since the soul emerges from it, our soul is something more. (M 20; AG 215)

Animals and human beings generally operate at the level of feeling and consciousness. Rocks and those things we normally consider inanimate never do.

The designation of degrees of conscious awareness is one of Leibniz's most significant innovations, and it is fundamental to almost every aspect of his account of monads. To understand the impetus behind it, we must consider how it arises from a conception of mind derived from Descartes. In discussing substance, along with the term 'mode', Descartes also discusses the term 'attribute'. A substance's attribute is its basic way of being. For Descartes, just as there are two basic kinds of substances, minds and bodies, there are two attributes – thought and extension. All modifications or qualities of a substance are modifications of its attribute. Thus all the properties of a body must be modifications of extension across space. Similarly, all the properties of a mind must be modifications of thought. That is, the only properties that minds have are thoughts or ideas. The current properties of any mind, then, are reducible to the current contents of its consciousness, in the same way that the current properties of any body are reducible to the way it currently takes up space. If we equate thought with what that mind is consciously aware of, several problems follow. First, if something is not consciously aware, it cannot be a mind. Thus rocks and trees cannot have minds, a point that Leibniz rejects. Second, if there are moments when a mind completely lacks awareness, as in a deep sleep or a coma, then at that moment, that mind does not exist. If the only properties of a mind are its conscious thoughts, then without conscious thought the mind has no properties and thus no existence. A mind without awareness would be like a body without extension. The obvious problem with this consequence is sleep. Either minds must have conscious awareness even in the deepest sleep, a point that Locke disputes, or minds go in and out of existence with their thoughts, a claim Leibniz attacks as a threat to the natural immortality of the soul. Third, there can be no ideas in a mind unless the mind is consciously aware of them. This conclusion has some strange consequences, for example, for the status of memory. If we are not aware of a memory, then it cannot be in our mind, but if it is not in a mind it must be in a body. Thus memories would continually have to shift from being modifications of extension across space to being modifications of consciousness. The deeper problem, though, is in relation to so-called 'innate ideas'. Innate ideas, such as the idea of God or a chiliagon, were thought to be naturally contained in all rational minds. The existence of innate ideas was central to the claim that not all knowledge comes from experience alone. This debate will be examined in more detail later, but if everything in a mind is in the mind's conscious awareness, then if some ideas are in the mind innately, it seems we must be always aware of them. Yet experience tells us that many people are not aware of these ideas, and that no one is continually aware of them.

The tensions in this view of mind are most clearly raised by John Locke. The foundation for his attack on innate knowledge, and thus the basis for his claim that all knowledge is learned from experience, rests on one principle – there can be nothing in the mind of which the mind is not consciously aware: 'To say a Notion is imprinted on the mind, and yet at the same time to say that the mind is ignorant of it, and never yet took notice of it is to make this Impression nothing. No Proposition can be said to be in the mind, which it never yet knew, which it was never yet conscious of'.[1] With this principle, Locke easily attacks innate ideas by arguing empirically that no ideas or principles are consciously recognized by all people. Thus there can be no knowledge that is innate to all minds. A corollary to the above principle is Locke's repeated claim that if something must be learned, it cannot be innate. Learning means bringing an idea into conscious awareness; if there is nothing in the mind of which we are not already aware, then ideas that are learned must come from outside the mind. They cannot be innate. Since we must learn things like geometry and even the concept of God, none of these can be innate. Locke takes both of these key principles for granted, offering no argument. He simply assumes that what it means to be in the mind is to be in the mind's conscious awareness. Leibniz's innovation is to deny that assumption. He explicitly argues that there are things in our minds of which we are not aware, calling these unrecognized perceptions 'minute perceptions' or 'petite perceptions'. The existence of minute perceptions allows Leibniz to give minds properties that are outside current awareness but not outside the mind itself.

The claim that there are parts of the mind to which we do not have conscious access no longer seems strange or surprising. The influence of a Freudian idea of the 'subconscious' runs so deep in modern thought that most people would now find Locke's position stranger than Leibniz's. To avoid confusion, though, a few aspects of Leibniz's account must be kept in mind. First, for Leibniz, a monad is one unitary mind. There is not one mind which is consciousness and then some other parallel mind which is the subconscious. The mind does not divide into two discrete regions. The difference between conscious thoughts and subconscious thoughts is not a difference in kind but a difference in degree: 'they are only less well distinguished and less developed because of their multiplicity' (WF 250). Thoughts exist on a continuum of clarity and distinctness. The fundamental difference between thoughts is not whether or not they are recognized but rather how strong they are. Leibniz calls unrecognized perceptions *minute* rather than *unconscious*, because they exist in our consciousness but are too faint to be recognized. Several consequences follow. First, much of our conscious experience results from the grouping together of minute perceptions. Minute perceptions are not in a separate subconscious region but rather are the components of our consciousness. The presence of minute perceptions in consciousness leads to a further point: that these perceptions exert some faint influence. These faint influences often conflict and negate each other, but they still play a key role in how we live. Every time we make a decision without deliberate consideration, even something as insignificant as whether to open a door with the left or right hand, that decision is determined by the conjunction of minute perceptions. As Leibniz puts it in a reply to Pierre Bayle:

> I have already shown more than once that the soul does many things without knowing how it does them – when it does them by means of confused perceptions and unconscious inclinations or appetites, of which there are always an extremely large number, so that it is impossible for the soul to be conscious of them, or to distinguish them clearly. (WF 238)

Leibniz's dependence on minute perceptions goes beyond the need to justify innate ideas and explain the mind-like existence of rocks. Each monad expresses the entire universe in its perception. Since we obviously are not *aware* of the entire universe, the great majority of our perceptions must exist below the level of conscious awareness. Thus the arguments discussed in chapter 3 simultaneously support and depend on the fact that monads have perceptions which are not apperceived. Furthermore, we have seen that variations in monads derive from their overall level of perfection and their particular perspective. Since all monads perceive the entire world, these differences are differences between perception and apperception, either in the ratio of one to the other or in what in particular is apperceived. Thus the relationship between perception and apperception is essential for understanding Leibniz's account of consciousness, pre-established harmony, and perspective. Leibniz provides a number of independent arguments for the existence of minute perceptions. These arguments appear most fully in the *New Essays on the Human Understanding*, a book

Leibniz wrote in direct response to Locke. One of those arguments points to the status of memory. Leibniz writes –

> Our gifted author seems to claim that there is nothing *implicit* in us, in fact nothing of which we are not always actually aware. But he cannot hold strictly to this; otherwise his position would be too paradoxical, since, again, we are not always aware of our acquired dispositions or of the contents of our memory, and they do not even come readily to mind whenever we need them, though often they come readily to mind when some idle circumstance reminds us of them, as when hearing the opening words of a song is enough to bring back the rest. (NE 52)

We are sometimes able to bring past experiences back into our awareness. These memories come from within our mind rather than from some external source, even if particular experiences are sometimes required to trigger them. It seems, then, that experiences remain in our minds as memories, even though we are usually not aware of them. In fact, we cannot even recall them at will. If the only qualities in a mind are perceptions, then memories must exist in our minds as thoughts or perceptions which are not apperceived. Again, though, the mind does not simply divide into two parts, consciousness and memory. Memories have a residual existence in the present moment, which Leibniz says retains 'traces' of the past. Otherwise, a current experience could not spontaneously arouse a memory. The accessibility of memories proves that they continue to have some faint, minute presence in consciousness. Since conscious awareness is a matter of degrees, Leibniz can easily account for the unrecognized influence of memory, as when we find ourselves liking someone and only later realize they remind us of an old friend, or when we come up with a 'new' idea later to realize we heard it from someone else. Leibniz explicitly mentions habit along with memory in the above passage. When we perform learned actions without an awareness of them or the process of having learning them, we again exhibit the unrecognized presence of memory in our current experience.

Leibniz's other arguments are primarily phenomenological, relying on careful observation of conscious experience. We have all had the experience of background music playing without our noticing it. If someone then comments on the song, we realize that we have been 'hearing' it all along (NE 54). In this situation, we move from a state of perception to one of apperception. Similarly, we sometimes find ourselves 'singing' a song in our mind and only then realize we heard that song in the background earlier without noticing, an experience which shows that such unnoticed perceptions can still have an influence. Leibniz's phenomenological arguments generally rely on two principles. One is another application of the principle of continuity. If something large has a noticeable impact on our consciousness, something small must also have an influence. Leibniz applies this principle to sleep, arguing that if we lacked a slight awareness of our environment while asleep, we could never be awoken. If a small amount of noise had no impact on our mind, how could a large amount of noise – basically a lot of small noise together – impact our mind? Leibniz compares this to tension on a rope. If a slight amount of tension did not strain the rope, a large amount of tension could not break the rope (NE 54). This principle underlies Leibniz's most common illustration of minute perceptions, the roar of the sea:

> To give a clearer idea of these minute perceptions which we are unable to pick out from the crowd, I like to use the example of the roaring noise of the sea which impresses itself on us when we are standing on the shore. To hear this noise as we do, we must hear the parts which make up this whole, that is the noise of each wave, although each of these little noises makes itself known only when combined confusedly with all the others, and would not be noticed if the wave which made it were by itself. We must be affected slightly by the motion of this wave, and have some perception of each of these noises, however faint they may be; otherwise there would be no perception of a hundred thousand waves, since a hundred thousand nothings cannot make something. (NE 54)

The same point is illustrated by the way a small change in degree can bring something into our awareness, as a small increase in the volume of a song makes it intrusive. That small amount of volume could not enter consciousness unless all of the volume it builds on were already somehow in consciousness. The second principle appeals to the inherent complexity of any moment of consciousness: 'There are hundreds of indications leading us to conclude that at every moment there is in us an infinity of perceptions' (NE 53). This point was already implicit in the earlier discussion of how consciousness contains a multiplicity in unity and how details emerge into awareness from a background of perception. Within the horizon of my consciousness, I can shift my focus from one object to another. I can attend to the details of the texture and colour of a certain table and then I can shift to focus on the wrinkles on the face of the person sitting at it. Surely those details are in some way already 'seen' by me, but without my notice. In fact, those details constitute the face I see, as I might think someone has a kind or attractive face without attending to the specific characteristics which generate that impression. The fact that I could attend to these details indicates that they are already present on some level, even if we never do attend to them. Leibniz illustrates this point by appeal to colour: ' [W]hen we perceive the color green in a mixture of yellow and blue powder, we sense only yellow and blue finely mixed, even though we do not notice this, but rather fashion some new thing for ourselves' (AG 27). The point is even clearer if we begin by imagining blue and yellow pebbles, which we would see as blue and yellow. As the size of those pebbles shrank, we would more and more just see the mixture as green. At some point, we might see it as green generally but blue and yellow when we attended to it carefully, just as we can hear the same music as a band or as four instruments, depending on how closely we attend to it.

This process can also be explained through our embodied relationship to the world. Due to the interconnection of things, even the smallest body has some effect on every other body. Thus my body receives the effects of every other body in the world. Obviously these effects cannot remain distinct even as they impact the body itself. Rather, they combine to have general effects on my body. Every individual wave causes some vibration in the ear, but they cannot there remain distinct. They blur together; that blur is expressed in consciousness as the roar of the sea. In a similar way, Leibniz begins his above analysis of green with a deeper point – the real foundation of the colour green is not the colours of blue and yellow but rather the interaction of light and various bodies, which are then brought together in my eyes. The infinitely fine movement of light is blurred in its contact with my eye, which is expressed in my conscious awareness as either the colours of blue and yellow or the colour of green. Just as point of view is located according to the position of our body, the distinctness of our perceptions expresses the structure of our body. Thus the distinction between animals and other monads corresponds to differences in their bodies:

> But when a monad has organs that are adjusted in such a way that, through them, there is a contrast and distinction among the impressions they receive, and consequently contrast and distinction between the perceptions that represent them [in the monad] (as, for example, when the rays of light are concentrated and act with greater force because of the shape of the eye's humor), then this may amount to *sensation* ... (PNG 4; AG 208)

The stupor of basic monads comes from the fact that their perceptions are all equal, because their body simply absorbs the impact of all others. The structure of animal bodies concentrates and heightens certain perceptions which can then be recognized.

These bodily explanations should not obscure the more fundamental claim that mind and body do not interact, that in these explanations Leibniz speaks as Copernicans speak of the rising sun. The body does not organize and focus the effects of the world into perceptions which it then slips into consciousness through a window. This analysis of the body is useful in explaining consciousness, though, because these bodily processes more clearly express the same process occurring in monads themselves. Thus the infinite vibrations of air that are blurred into a pattern by the ear all exist as unrecognized perceptions in consciousness itself. Due to the interconnection of things and the containment of the whole universe within each monad, everything has some impact on consciousness. Those things that are closest, like the vibrations of air caused by a symphony performing in front of us, stand out from the dull hum of the rest of the universe. These vibrations, though, are still too faint to be recognized. They become confused into the sounds of the different instruments, which are further confused to become the sound of the symphony we actually hear. If we are attentive enough, from this confusion we might pick out some of the distinct instruments. In any case, we do sense them – if we didn't hear each instrument, we would not hear the symphony at all, just as if we did not perceive each vibration of air we would not perceive any sound. What we do not recognize in the music can even cause us pleasure. Leibniz describes the pleasures of music as an unconscious or 'occult' mathematics:

> I have shown elsewhere that the confused perception of plea-santness or unpleasantness which we find in consonances or dissonances consists in an occult arithmetic. The soul counts the beats of the vibrating object which makes the sound, and when these beats regularly coincide at short intervals, it finds them pleasing. Thus it counts without knowing it. (WF 238)

Leibniz's account of the composition of apperception by an infinity of unrecognized perceptions has several significant conse-quences for his theory of knowledge, particular for his account of sensory perception. Most of these arise through disputes with Locke. Locke takes sensory impressions as the fundamental building blocks of thought. He takes them as simple – a colour just is what it is, it has no parts and is not derived from something more simple. We combine these simple sensory ideas together to form complex ideas, as the idea of a table is a combination of the simple impressions of its colour, texture, and so on.[2] While Leibniz would agree that the table can be analysed according to various sensory impressions, that analysis should not end with colour:

> It can be maintained, I believe, that these sensible ideas appear simple because they are confused and thus do not provide the mind with any way of making discriminations within what they contain; just like distant things appear rounded because one cannot discern their angles, even though one is receiving some confused impression from them. It is obvious that green, for instance, comes from a mixture of blue and yellow; which makes it credible that the idea of green is composed of the ideas of those two colours, although the idea of green appears to us as simple as that of blue, or as that of warmth. (NE 120)

In this passage, Leibniz uses 'idea' in the broad sense of percep-tion. The perception of a colour is composite, not simple, as is clear with the case of green as a mix of blue and yellow. The fact that colours *appear* simple is just a sign of how confused they are. Consequently, the analysis of experience must go beyond reduction to sensory impressions. We can analyse the symphony into its instruments and analyse those into vibrations of air, but given the infinite divisibility of matter, our analysis can continue to infinity. We can analyse air into its component molecules, analyse those into their parts, and so on. Leibniz's account has a further advantage over that of Locke. If sensory perceptions are simple, as Locke argues, then they seem incommensurate with the physical world itself. The physical world is determined by the movement of infinitely divisible matter – how could such a world produce simple unanalysable colours? That is, to maintain a coherent relationship between sense perception and the world itself, sense perceptions must be as complex as the world itself. The problem is heightened if we take colour as existing on the level of mind and all the rest as existing in the world of body, as Locke does. Lacking a coherent way to account for either the relation of mind and body or how an infinitely complex physical movement could generate an absolutely simple sensation, Locke claims that sensations like colour, smell, and sound have only an arbitrary connection to the world. Leibniz instead says that, 'every feeling is the perception of a truth' (NE 94). The sound of a symphony is composed of other perceptions just as the movement of the ear drum is composed of the infinite vibrations of air. The contours of conscious awareness differ greatly from the infinite complexity of the world, but perception directly expresses that infinity. Leibniz once again employs the concept of expression:

> It must not be thought that ideas such as those of colour and pain are arbitrary and that between them and their causes there is no relation or natural connection: it is not God's way to act in such an unruly and unreasoned fashion. I would say, rather, that there is a resemblance of a kind – not a perfect one which holds all the way through, but a resemblance in which one thing expresses another through some orderly relationship between them. (NE 131).

It is a little ironic that Leibniz, usually labelled a 'Rationalist', puts more truth in sensory perception than Locke the 'Empiricist', but this only supports a point that has already appeared several times: Leibniz's philosophy largely serves to justify and enable a coherent empirical account of the world. This point also shows how the labels 'Rationalist' and 'Empiricist' can be misleading. The difference between Locke and Leibniz is not based on how seriously they take experience; Leibniz takes it at least as seriously and he is much more concerned with science. The real contrast is around the status and role of reason, a contrast that will be more clear in the following section.

The grounding of conscious awareness in an infinite complexity of perceptions that can never be analysed into absolutely simple parts sets the direction for Leibniz's entire account of knowledge. We can see this direction once again through a contrast with Locke. For Locke, the fundamental epistemological issues centre on *construction*. We begin with simple unanalysable ideas. Our one task is to increase those simple ideas through experience. Our other task is to properly combine them into complex ideas. Thus Locke describes various faculties and principles for putting simple ideas into proper combinations, for example, connecting ideas based on similarity or proximity in space or time. Leibniz's approach comes from the opposite direction. Our basic condition is not as a blank tablet whose content needs to be written and composed; on the contrary, our basic condition is to be over-whelmed with information. We always already express an infi-nitely detailed universe from a finite perspective. The primary task then is not to compose complex ideas from simple ones but rather to make some sense of the already composed and complex contents of our conscious awareness. We must sort through these perceptions, attend to them in more detail, pick out patterns in them, find analogies between patterns. Thus, the primary episte-mological task is not construction but *analysis*. This process of analysis is never complete and we never arrive at simples which fully explain consciousness itself. The question of how to organize experience can only be a question of how to better organize it, since consciousness is always already organized. The goal of knowledge is not immediately to give order to perceptions but first to illuminate the order already implicit in experience. We begin with the complex perception of the symphony and our pleasure in it. From there, we can build knowledge by attempting to distinguish the various instruments we already hear without recognition or to make explicit the mathematics that we already perform without awareness.

II. NECESSARY TRUTHS AND INNATE IDEAS

Leibniz grounds the distinction between animals and other monads in the fact that animal souls can recognize and retain their perceptions. The difference between human animals and other animals partly lies in the greater distinctness of human perception, but the difference is more radical than just a greater degree of clarity. Leibniz introduces this difference through the ways in which experiences are linked together:

> There is interconnection among the perceptions of animals which bears some resemblance to reason, but this interconnection is only founded in the memory of *facts* or effects, and not at all in the knowledge of *causes*. That is why a dog runs away from the stick with which he was beaten, because his memory represents to him the pain which the stick caused him. And men, to the extent that they are empirical, that is, in three fourths of their actions, act only like beasts. For example, we expect the day to dawn tomorrow because we have always experienced it thus; only an astronomer foresees it by reason, and even this prediction will finally fail, when the cause of the dawning, which is not eternal, shall cease. But *true reasoning* depends on necessary and eternal truths, such as those of logic, numbers, and geometry, which bring about an indubitable connection of ideas and infallible consequences. Animals in which these consequences are not noticed are called *beasts*; but those who know these necessary truths are those that are properly called *rational animals*, and their souls are properly called minds. (PNG 5; AG 208–9)

Both animals and humans have a capacity for memory, which allows us all to link experiences together based on either the repetition or intensity of an experience. If two experiences often follow each other, then when we experience one, we expect the other. In many cases, we can rely on these expectations, as we rely on the daily rising of the sun. Beyond this linking of experience, though, human beings also can attain *causal knowledge*, which allows them to know that from one experience another experience *must* follow, necessarily. We can know *why* one event follows another, as the astronomer knows why the sun continues to move and what factors might alter its movement. Causal knowledge involves necessary connections between events; it involves a grasp of necessary and eternal truths, based ultimately on the principle of non-contradiction.

These necessary truths cannot derive from experience. Truths from experience are derived by induction from repeated instances of experience. No matter how often a link between experiences is repeated, we can at most know that in the future this connection will be extremely likely: 'however many instances confirm a general truth, they do not suffice to establish its universal necessity; for it does not follow that what has happened will always happen in the same way' (NE 49). In part, this limitation follows from the limitation of any one perspective. Leibniz sometimes refers to a story he heard about the King of Siam. Among all the things the Europeans told him, the most difficult to believe was that water could take the form of ice, since no one in his kingdom had ever experienced it (NE 433–4). On a deeper level, the very existence of this particular world is only a contingent fact. God could have chosen a different world. Thus experience can teach us what this world happens to be like, but it can never tell us the way things necessarily must be. As often as it is repeated, the rising of the sun is a contingent fact about this particular world, and some day the rising of the sun may end. Consider Leibniz's paradigm for necessary truths: geometry. We know the properties of a triangle with much greater certainty than we could ever attain by measuring triangular things in the world. No matter how many triangles we measured, we could only know that in all of the ones we came across, the angles added up to roughly 180 degrees. We could never know if this fact were universal or only a constant fact about our own perspective, like the constant liquidity of water in the perspective of the King of Siam.

Consequently, access to necessary truths cannot come through an increase in the distinctness of our expression of the contingent, created world. It requires another source, accessible only to rational minds. That source is God. In the *Monadology*, Leibniz writes, 'souls, in general, are living mirrors or images of the universe of creatures, but minds are also images of the divinity itself, or of the author of nature' (M 83; AG 223; cf. PNG 14; AG 211). In the *Discourse on Metaphysics*, Leibniz connects this difference to the greater value of human beings:

> [A] single mind is worth a whole world, since it does not merely express the world but it also knows it and it governs itself after the fashion of God. In this way we may say that, although all substances express the whole universe, nevertheless the other substances express the world rather than God, while minds express God rather than the world. (DM 36; AG 67)

All monads ultimately express God, both in the general way that any effect expresses its cause and more specifically as an expression of a universe that itself expresses God's wisdom, goodness, and power. Nonetheless, human beings also have a direct relationship to God, expressing God's understanding directly. We have already seen that the necessity of God's nature requires that his understanding contain all possible thoughts, every idea which is not internally contradictory. Among these are an infinity of contingent truths, including the ideas of all possible worlds, and all necessary truths, such as the truths of mathematics or truths about the nature of substance. God thinks all of these truths in all possible ways, so God's understanding also contains ideas of relationships and of abstractions and generalities. That is, God not only has an idea of every possible human being, but also an idea of 'human being' in general, as we have seen. The reality of such abstract concepts and relations ultimately depends on their existence in God: 'The reality of relations is dependent on mind, as is that of truths; but they do not depend on the human mind, as there is a supreme intelligence which determines all of them from all time' (NE 265). Every thing that exists is a particular substance, so relations and abstractions like 'human being' have no referent in created things. Yet because relations and general ideas are contained in the mind of God, they are neither arbitrary nor mere human constructs.

Human beings have access to these necessary truths because they express not only the created universe but also the understanding of God. In connecting necessary truths to God, Leibniz follows a long tradition that begins with Plato, is Christianized by Augustine, and enters the early modern period through Descartes.

The connection may now seem strange, but it follows from the characteristics of this kind of truth. Truths such as those of mathematics seem to be necessary and eternal, applying not only to our world but to the way any world could possibly be. Descartes claims they even apply in dreams. The only thing whose existence and nature is necessary and eternal, though, is God, making God the only possible ground for such truths. Leibniz takes our grasp of necessary truths as proof for the existence of a necessary God, as we have seen. This connection to God aligns with the common claim that human beings and human beings alone are made in the image of God, a phrase Leibniz himself uses in the passage above. If our most distinctive feature is our use of reason, then it follows that reason belongs to and is derived from God. The most immediate precursor to Leibniz's position is that of Nicolas Malebranche. Developing a line of thought from Augustine, Malebranche argued that we see ideas in the mind of God. That is, the ideas I have of necessary truths are never really contained in my mind; rather, when I contemplate them I access something in the mind of God itself.[3] Leibniz claimed that Malebranche's position followed from a misunderstanding of the nature of substance, which has no windows and must already contain all of its perceptions and ideas. He writes,

> As to the controversy over whether or not we see everything in God (which is certainly an old opinion and should not be rejected completely, if it is understood properly) or whether we have our own ideas, one must understand that, even if we were to see everything in God, it would nevertheless be necessary that we also have our own ideas, that is, not little copies of God's, as it were, but affections or modifications of our mind corresponding to that very thing we perceived in God. (AG 27)

The position of Malebranche is not entirely wrong, if understood properly. We 'perceive' ideas in the mind of God in exactly the same sense that we 'perceive' the rest of the universe. Leibniz consistently describes both relationships in the same terms. In both cases, monads do not interact and take in new ideas or perceptions; rather these ideas and perceptions unfold from within each monad. The structure and truth of those thoughts, however, lie in what they express, either the created universe or the mind of God.

One of the central debates in the early modern period was between those who claimed that all knowledge comes from experience and those who claimed that some knowledge is innate. This debate largely defines the line between those now labelled as 'Rationalists' and those labelled as 'Empiricists'. Innate ideas developed largely as a default category for ideas that we have but do not seem to be derived from experience. They can be divided into three overlapping groups. The first are ideas that can only be learned through self-reflection, such as the idea of perception or will. We only know these as they exist in ourselves. These ideas still arise from experience, but from the experience of our own consciousness. Leibniz appeals to them occasionally as examples of innate ideas, as when he claims that the idea of a unitary substance is innate because it is only reached by reflection on our consciousness. Since these ideas still come through experience, though, they are accepted by Locke as well, who distinguishes two kinds of experience, experience of the world and experience of reflection.[4] The second group are ideas from which we derive necessary truths, like the idea of a perfect triangle. As we have seen, experience only gives us particular cases, so ideas that derive from experience cannot generate necessary truths. Thus while experience might lead us to consider geometry, geometrical truths cannot be derived from experience itself. The third category includes ideas that structure experience rather than derive from experience. For example, substance seems to be an idea that organizes experience – the idea of separate, stable substances would never occur to us if all we had was the immediate flux of interconnected perceptions. Another example is the truth that something cannot come from nothing, which leads to the truth that every effect must have a cause. We do not learn this from experience, since we often experience things that have no apparent cause. Rather, we assume this principle in order to make sense of experience in the first place. In a broad sense, the mind itself must have some innate ability to organize and make sense of the flux of perception. This ability falls into the category of innate ideas because on the Cartesian conception of mind, the only properties of a mind are its thoughts or ideas, as we have seen. Any property of a mind must be an idea.

On one level, the debate around innate ideas has little relevance to Leibniz. Nothing new ever enters a monad, so strictly speaking all of our ideas and perceptions are innate. Nonetheless, the distinction between what comes from a monad's expression of the universe and what comes from its expression of God maps on to the distinction between ideas from experience and ideas that are innate. Ideas that express the mind of God fill all three of the above-mentioned roles usually performed by innate ideas. Leibniz explicitly enters the debate around innate ideas through his criticisms of Locke. In the *New Essays*, he explains his position:

> I believe indeed that all the thoughts and actions of our soul come from its own depths and could not be given to it by the senses. But in the meantime I shall set aside the inquiry into that, and shall conform to accepted ways of speaking, since they are indeed sound and justifiable. ... I shall thus work within the common framework, speaking of the action of the body on the soul, in the way that the Copernicans quite justifiably join other men in talking about the movement of the sun; and I shall look into why, even within this framework, one should in my opinion say that there are ideas and principles which do not reach us through the senses, and which we find in ourselves without having formed them, though the senses bring them into our awareness. (NE 74)

We have already seen the basis for both Locke's argument against innate ideas and Leibniz's response. On one side, Locke relies on his principles that there is nothing in the mind of which we are not aware and that if something is learned it cannot be innate. On these principles, if there were ideas innate to all rational minds, then all human beings would have to be consciously aware of them all of the time. Since there are no such universally recognized ideas, there can be no universally innate ideas. Leibniz's doctrine of minute perceptions replies to this argument. On the other side, Locke argues that if all ideas can be accounted for by experience, then there is no need to posit an additional innate source of ideas. Much of his *An Essay Concerning Human Understanding* is directed toward showing how all of our ideas can be derived from and explained by experience. Leibniz responds to this approach by pointing out various kinds of ideas that we have but that cannot come from experience, using all three of the above-mentioned categories of innate ideas. His focus, though, is on necessary truths or principles. After arguing that experience only gives us contingent truths, Leibniz concludes:

> From this it appears that necessary truths, such as those we find in pure mathematics and particularly in arithmetic and geometry, must have principles whose proof does not depend on instances nor, consequently, on the testimony of the senses, even though without the senses it would never occur to us to think of them. (NE 50)

Leibniz has some difficulty articulating the form these innate ideas have in a mind, using a number of different terms: inclinations, dispositions, habits, aptitudes. An innate idea marks an active tendency toward conscious awareness of an idea already contained in us. The role of innate ideas can be clarified by analogy with memories. Memories are ideas that exist as perceptions in the mind, but go unrecognized most of the time. At the same time, they have a trace existence in every moment of consciousness and thus can exert an effect, even if we are usually unaware of that effect or its cause. Innate ideas function in a similar way. They exist outside conscious awareness, but they have a trace effect on every moment of consciousness. This trace allows us to bring them to our explicit attention and even constitutes a natural tendency toward using them. Even when unrecognized, these ideas influence our experience. When Locke argues that very few people recognize the principle of contradiction, Leibniz replies that fundamentally everyone knows it and uses it all the time but without having the principle explicitly in mind. When we recognize that someone is lying because they contradict themselves, we implicitly use the principle of contradiction, which tells us that contradictory claims cannot both be true (NE 76). Leibniz explains:

> For general principles enter into our thoughts, serving as their inner core and as their mortar. Even if we give no thought to them, they are necessary for thought, as muscles and tendons are for walking. The mind relies on these principles constantly; but it does not find it so easy to sort them out and to command a distinct view of them separately, for that requires

great attention to what one is doing, and the unreflective majority are hardly capable of that. (NE 84)

In a similar way, we organize the world into 'things', implicitly using the concept of substance without thinking about the nature of substance itself, just as we instinctively link events by cause and effect without considering the principle of sufficient reason. We can see again how the focus of learning for Leibniz is on analysis – uncovering and clarifying what is already implicit in us. We can indeed learn things that are already in us, bringing them from perception into apperception. This process of clarification eventually leads to the two principles which found all knowledge – the principle of contradiction and the principle of sufficient reason. We began by noting that Leibniz gives no clear proof for these principles but rather takes them as implicit in any attempt to establish the truth. We can now see more concretely what that means. We already accept and use both principles – our entire conscious experience is structured by them. They exist as the implicit ordering of our engagement with the world, our ability to recognize contradictions and to link events causally. Yet the principles themselves must be uncovered.

Leibniz says that rational minds *express* the ideas in the mind of God, the same term he uses to describe the relationship between monads and the created universe. In both cases, something infinite is expressed in something finite, necessitating limitations in that expression. Since the created universe is infinitely complex, both as infinitely divisible and as infinitely interrelated, any expression of it in a finite monad will be more or less confused. Analysis never reaches utterly clear and distinct elements of perception – analysis continues to infinity. The order and connection of these perceptions correlates to or expresses the order and connection of things themselves, but much of this order is hidden in confusion, a point Leibniz uses in arguing against our ability to judge empirically the perfection of this world. In contrast, the ideas we have as expressions of God are abstract and relatively simple, making them much easier to grasp. We can grasp the essence of an abstract triangle in a more complete way than the essence of a particular triangular piece of wood, which has a contingent history and complex material. Innate ideas – that is, those ideas which we have as expressions of the mind of God – can be clearly and distinctly understood and can be known with complete certainty. Leibniz says: 'All reasonings are eminent in God, and they preserve an order among themselves in his understanding as well as in ours; but for him this is just an order and a priority of nature, whereas for us there is a priority of time' (NE 396). We have already seen the crucial role this commonality plays in Leibniz's philosophy, particularly in relation to his conception of God and his ethical and political theories. The limitation of a finite mind, though, means we can only grasp a limited number of necessary truths. This limitation is expressed by the limitations of time. While we can know necessary truths with certainty, the limitation of time fundamentally shapes human experience and generates some of Leibniz's main practical concerns. In the very process of reasoning, the limitation of time means that we cannot hold together too many truths at once. Complex chains of reasoning depend on memory and signs. In addition, no matter how much time we have, we can only discover a small number of these necessary truths; which particular truths we come to discover depends on our particular course of study. This necessary limit makes exchange and interaction crucial, as Leibniz himself recognized and addressed in both his writings and his political efforts. He facilitated this exchange himself through his immense correspondence and his support of learned societies, extending it all the way to cultural exchange with China, which he calls a 'commerce of light'. This concern with exchange reflects the limited ability any one person has to discover even necessary truths.

On a deeper level, although minds rely on two radically separate sources of knowledge – the expression of God and the expression of the created world – those do not lead to a split in conscious experience. We do not make some radical switch from one to the other. Innate ideas are integrated into a particular point of view, which is expressed through embodiment in a particular world. The two expressions are mutually shaping. Our conscious experience is fundamentally structured according to necessary truths and innate ideas. This structure includes seeing the world in terms of distinct things (relying on an innate idea of substance), expecting that any event will have a cause and organizing events into causal chains (implicitly using the principle of sufficient reason), and rejecting contradictions as false (using the principle of non-contradiction). In the other direction, one of the main limitations on our grasp of necessary truths are the demands of embodied life – we must spent most of our time in the practical pursuits required for staying alive. For Leibniz, the pursuit of knowledge requires some leisure and must go along with a reduction in more materialistic desires (NE 87). More importantly, the truths we uncover depend on our particular cultural, linguistic, and historical contexts. Leibniz takes all of these factors much more seriously than his contemporaries. He does not believe that necessary truths originate from culture or history, both of which are contingent, but that the movement of necessary truths into conscious awareness depends on cultural and historical situation. In other words, experience does not create innate ideas but it provides the occasions that prompt the consideration of those ideas. For example, truths of geometry in no way depend on culture. They are necessary, eternal, and universal, contained innately in all human minds and grounded in the necessary structure of God's understanding. Nonetheless, learning those truths – bringing them into apperception – depends on how much leisure we have and on who teaches us geometry. Leibniz writes:

> As for the proposition that every man has a notion of God, if 'notion' signifies an idea then that is a proposition of reason, because in my view the idea of God is innate in all men. But if 'notion' signifies an idea which involves actual thinking, then it is a proposition of fact, belonging to the natural history of mankind. (NE 430)

The distinction Leibniz makes in this passage is between the innate ideas implicit in every rational monad and those thoughts that particular minds actually become aware of. In other words, it is a distinction between perception and apperception. The latter depends on the 'natural history of mankind', that is, on culture. This greater awareness of our dependence on culture and history lies behind Leibniz's concern with language, his promotion of exchange with China, and his more serious engagement with the history of philosophy.

III. KNOWLEDGE

The pursuit of knowledge has several interrelated directions for Leibniz. On one side, we need to analyse our perceptions into greater and greater detail, making them more and more distinct, as colours are analysed into the qualities of light. This process has no end because existing things are infinitely complex. On the other side, we must organize these perceptions, particularly by connecting them into causal chains, the ability that most distinguishes human beings from other animals. This process consists of uncovering and clarifying the principles that we already implicitly use, then consciously using these principles to organize our experience more coherently. Although these innate ideas can be known with complete certainty, this process of discovery also is unending, as experience leads us to uncover and clarify more and more innate ideas. Ultimately, the search for truth generates a dialectical or reciprocal process. By analysing our particular judgements, we come to grasp more clearly the principles we implicitly use. With these principles clarified, we can better organize and clarify experience itself, which in turn allows us to recognize more of those implicit principles.

Reasoning in its purest form consists in the use of innate ideas and necessary truths. Leibniz defines reasoning as linking truths according to their necessary connections. From the concept-containment theory – that every idea contains all of its predicates – reasoning can just as well be described as the analysis of complex ideas into their necessary components. In discussing the analysis of ideas, Leibniz takes a phrase from Descartes while shifting its meaning. The phrase he uses is *clear and distinct*. In the second meditation, Descartes writes, 'So I now seem to be able to lay it down as a general rule that whatever I perceive very clearly and distinctly is true.'[5] Descartes does not give a criterion for recognizing clarity and distinctness, but gives an example: clarity and distinctness describe the way that I know that I exist. Clarity and distinctness describe a way of grasping an idea that is so forceful – so clear and distinct – that it cannot but be believed. For Descartes, although we cannot really doubt ideas grasped in this way, their truth is only fully established with the proof for the existence of God. A good God would not make human beings such that they felt so compelled to believe things that were false. Setting aside the problems with using God to guarantee truth, the problem in Descartes' account is how to recognize when an idea is truly clear and distinct. How do we distinguish those ideas that we cannot doubt because they are deep prejudices from those ideas we cannot doubt because they are clear and distinct? Descartes' response to this problem is complex and more plausible than it may initially seem, but his basic claim is that once we experience a clear and distinct idea, we will be able to recognize how it differs from blind prejudice. Many of Descartes' contemporaries and immediate successors rejected clarity and distinctness as too subjective. Concern about the misuse of these criteria lies behind Locke's attack on innate ideas. For Locke, innate ideas and claims to clarity and distinctness only excuse laziness and dogmatism. For any principle that is questioned, one can respond that the principle is innate and known clearly and distinctly. Nothing more can be said and nothing more can be demanded. Locke responds by rejecting innate ideas completely, so that any prejudice or assumption can be questioned by reducing it to its source in experience. We have already seen why Leibniz opposes Locke's solution, but he is sympathetic to Locke's criticism:

> I suppose that your able author [Locke] has been made hostile to the doctrine of innate principles because he has noticed that people often maintain their prejudices under the name of innate principles, wanting to excuse themselves from the trouble of discussing them. He will have wanted to fight the laziness and the shallowness of thought of those who use the specious pretext of innate ideas and truths, naturally engraved on the mind and readily assented to, to avoid serious inquiry into where our items of knowledge come from, how they are connected, and what certainty they have. I am entirely on his side about that, and I would go even further. I would like no limits to be set to our analysis, definitions to be given of all terms which admit of them, and demonstrations – or the means for them – to be provided for all axioms which are not primary, without reference to men's opinions about them and without caring whether they agree to them or not. (NE 74–5)

How many people accept a truth or how easily they accept it, even how certain they feel about it, all cannot be used to judge if a principle is *true*. Like Locke, Leibniz believes that ideas must be subject to analysis. Unlike Locke, this is not an analysis into basic sensory impressions, which themselves must be subjected to analysis.

In a sense, the purpose of reasoning is to draw out the consequences of and relationships between ideas. This process, though,
requires that the ideas we analyse not contain hidden contradictions. While Descartes thinks the validity of an idea can be determined by immediate experience, from the experience of clarity and
distinctness, Leibniz is less optimistic. The mutual implication of
experience and innate ideas, along with the necessary limits of any
finite perspective, often make it impossible to determine the clarity
and distinctness of an idea from immediate experience. The crucial
distinction Leibniz uses is one that has already appeared, between
a concept or notion and an idea. 'Concept' refers to an actual
thought in my conscious awareness; 'idea' refers to those thoughts
that are in me as an expression of the understanding of God.
While ideas are universal, innate, and contained equally in
everyone, thoughts or concepts arise through particular chains of
experience according to a particular point of view. Concepts can
be more or less clear and distinct. Since innate ideas express ideas
in the mind of God, they cannot contain contradictions. Contradictions are not only impossible in existence; they are impossible
to think, even for God. The problem, then, is not that innate
ideas can be false and so must be evaluated – all innate ideas
express God and must be true. The problem is that we cannot
easily distinguish between a confused concept/notion and a true
idea:

> Now, it is evident that we have no idea of a notion when it is
> impossible. And in the case where knowledge is only *supposi-
> tive*, even when we have the idea, we do not contemplate it, for
> such a notion is only known in the way in which we know
> notions involving a hidden impossibility; and if a notion is
> possible, we do not learn its possibility in this way. (DM 25;
> AG 57)

We cannot know that a notion is an idea, that is, that it expresses
something possible and thus contained in the mind of God,
simply through contemplation. Unlike ideas, notions or concepts
can be false. Leibniz clarifies these issues by applying them to Descartes' use of the ontological proof for the existence of God, discussed in chapter 2. Descartes argued that existence is a necessary
predicate of the idea of God. The idea of God is innate and when

I grasp it clearly and distinctly I know without doubt that God actually exists. Leibniz replies that this argument only works if we can first demonstrate that the idea of God is possible. In other words, Descartes must demonstrate that his *notion* of God is truly an *idea*. Leibniz offers the notion of the greatest speed as a comparison. He first shows that this notion represents something impossible – there can be no greatest speed because for any speed we can conceive one greater. He then continues:

> In spite of all that, we think about this greatest speed, something that has no idea since it is impossible. Similarly, the greatest circle of all is an impossible thing, and the number of all possible units is no less so; we have a demonstration of this. And nevertheless, we think about all this. That is why there are surely grounds for wondering whether we should be careful about the idea of the greatest of all beings, and whether it might not contain a contradiction. For I fully understand, for example, the nature of motion and speed and what it is to be greatest, but, for all that, I do not understand whether all those notions are compatible, and whether there is a way of joining them and making them into an idea of the greatest speed of which motion is capable. (AG 238)

In a sense, all of our perceptions and ideas are expressions of either God or the universe and in this sense they all have some truth. A false concept is really a confused thought that unites two incompatible ideas, such as speed and fastest. This confusion results from the necessary limits of any finite perspective. The key point is that this confusion cannot necessarily be recognized immediately and intuitively. It can only be recognized by analysis of a notion into its component ideas.

Leibniz's clearest account of the analysis of ideas is in an essay called 'Meditations on Knowledge, Truth and Ideas', which he published in 1684 but continued to cite throughout his life. In that essay, Leibniz discusses four distinctions. Thinking is either clear or obscure; clear knowledge is either distinct or confused; distinct knowledge is either adequate or inadequate; adequate knowledge is either intuitive or symbolic. We can briefly go through each of these distinctions. A notion is *obscure* if I cannot use it to recognize what it represents. Leibniz gives the example of a memory of a flower that is so vague it would not serve to distinguish that kind of flower from other similar ones. One could still think of the flower, but only in an obscure way. A notion is *clear*, then, when it suffices for recognizing its object. Clear notions, though, can be distinct or confused. A notion is *confused* when I lack explicit criteria for distinguishing it from others. I can recognize the idea intuitively, but cannot explain how I recognize it. Leibniz gives colour as an example – I know red when I see it but I could not give a criterion for recognizing red, as I could not explain red to someone who was blind. What Locke takes as the simple empirical ideas that form the basis of all thought, Leibniz takes as clear but confused ideas. For Leibniz, red is complex and can be analysed, but its components are not perceived distinctly, giving the illusion of simplicity.

A notion is clear and *distinct* when we can recognize it and make explicit the marks by which it is recognized. In other words, a clear and distinct idea can be defined. Leibniz gives as an example the idea an assayer has of gold – he or she has specific tests and criteria for distinguishing gold from other things. Geometrical figures are also clear and distinct, as they can be defined and recognized. Clarity and distinctness, though, are not sufficient for judging the truth of a notion. We need to analyse the components of that notion. If a notion itself is clear and distinct, then we must be able recognize its components, since these are the marks by which we define that notion. So in order to define gold, the assayer must recognize its distinguishing marks, such as its yellow colour, but these marks themselves are not necessarily clear and distinct, as the assayer can define gold but cannot define the yellow colour that is part of gold's definition. A distinct idea is *adequate* when both the idea and all of its components are known clearly and distinctly. Leibniz uses numbers as an example of adequate knowledge, but adds that there may be no perfectly adequate knowledge. That reflects his tendency to see analysis as an unending process and to view clarity and distinctness as a matter of degrees. We can see how Leibniz's criticism of Descartes fits in here. From Leibniz's perspective, Descartes stops too early, at clarity and distinctness, without examining the components of ideas. The idea of God is clear and distinct, since we can recognize and define it, but unless its components are also clear and distinct, we cannot be sure they are compatible.

In a sense, adequate knowledge is perfect knowledge. If we have a clear and distinct idea and clear and distinct ideas of all of its components, then we can be sure that the idea does not contain any contradictions hidden in obscurity. Even so, an idea can be known as adequate in two ways. Human minds are limited in how many ideas they can consider at once. Consciousness always contains a multiplicity, so we are able to hold some ideas together in our awareness, seeing their relations and compatibility. Leibniz calls this kind of adequate knowledge *intuitive*. It is immediately seen. Usually, though, we cannot hold an idea and all of its components in our attention at once; the scope of our awareness is too narrow. We must first analyse one component, then another, then another. Similarly, we can rarely use an idea while also considering all of its parts. In these cases, knowledge is not intuitive but rather *symbolic* or *blind*. Leibniz explains:

> However, we don't usually grasp the entire nature of a thing all at once, especially in a more lengthy analysis, but in place of the things themselves we make use of signs, whose explicit explanation we usually omit for the sake of brevity, knowing or believing that we have the ability to produce it at will. And so when I think about a chiliagon, that is, a polygon with a thousand equal sides, I don't always consider the nature of a side, or of equality, or of thousandfoldness (that is, of the cube of tenfoldedness), but in my mind I use these words (whose sense appears only obscurely and imperfectly to the mind) in place of the ideas I have of these things, since I remember that I know the meaning of those words, and I decide that explanation is not necessary at this time. I usually call such thinking, which is found both in algebra and in arithmetic and, indeed, almost everywhere, blind or symbolic. (AG 24–5)

Perfect knowledge is both adequate and intuitive. Under those conditions of analysis, we can be sure that a notion contains no hidden contradictions. That is, we can ensure that it represents something that is possible, thus something that is contained in the understanding of God, and thus is truly an idea.

Intuitive knowledge is extremely rare. Consider Leibniz's example of the chiliagon. To know it adequately requires not only analysing all of its component ideas, like 'side' and 'thousandfoldness', but also all the components of those components, until absolutely simple ideas are reached; for that knowledge to be intuitive, that whole analysis must be held together in the mind at the same time. Probably, this would be impossible; certainly, we could never do much geometry in this way. We must rely on blind and symbolic thought. This reliance is even deeper in longer demonstrations that rely on memory:

> The fact is that our systematic knowledge, even of the most demonstrative sort, since it very often has to be gained through a long chain of reasoning, must involve the recollection of a past demonstration which is no longer kept distinctly in mind once the conclusion is reached – otherwise we would be continually repeating the demonstration. Even while it is going on we cannot grasp the whole of it all at once, since its parts cannot be simultaneously present to the mind; and if we continually called the preceding part back into view we would never reach the final one which yields the conclusion. This has the further implication that without writing it would be difficult to get the sciences properly established, since memory is not certain enough. (NE 358–9)

Blind symbolic thought is necessary but it always introduces the possibility of error. The combination of our dependence on signs and the inherent risks involved with that dependence lead Leibniz to take the proper use of language, logic, and signs – what we could broadly call semiology – as one of the most important tasks for the progress of knowledge.

Blind thought can be taken as thought that uses words rather than ideas. We reason with words while not attending to the ideas they represent. This connection to language appears in the above example of the chiliagon and appears in Leibniz's discussion of the analysis of notions. Thus the process of analysis is also a process of definition. To render an idea clear, distinct, and adequate is to give that notion what Leibniz calls a *real definition*. A real definition proves the possibility of what it defines by breaking it down into simple ideas. In contrast, when a notion is only clear and distinct, we have a *nominal definition*, a definition that allows us to distinguish the notion from others but does not establish the possibility of what the notion represents. We could give a nominal definition of the fastest motion, a definition that allows us to recognize that notion, but we could not give it a real definition. The attempt would reveal that the notion itself is contradictory. This focus on the role of definition in the process of analysis reflects the degree to which reasoning depends on words. Leibniz discusses the foundations of language in a brief dialogue that addresses Hobbes.[6] Leibniz begins by agreeing that truth and falsity apply to propositions, not things themselves. That is, a thing cannot be false; only statements about it can be false. He also argues that all propositions involve language or signs, claiming that we could not do maths without numerical signs and that even geometry relies on signs, as we use the figure of a circle to represent a true circle. From these points, the dialogue takes up the main difficulty:

A. Certain learned men [Hobbes] think that truth arises from decisions people make, and from names or characters.
B. This view is quite paradoxical.
A. But they prove it in this way: Isn't a definition the starting place for a demonstration?
B. I admit that it is, for some propositions can be demonstrated only from definitions joined to one another.
A. Therefore, the truth of such propositions depends on definitions.
B. I concede that.
A. But definitions depend on our decision.
B. How so?
A. Don't you see that it is a matter of decision among mathematicians to use the word 'ellipse' in such a way that it signifies a particular figure? Or that it was a matter of decision among the Latins to impose on the word 'circulus' the meaning that the definition expresses? (AG 270)

Leibniz recognizes that there is no similarity between the group of letters 'c-i-r-c-l-e' and that round figure we use it to represent, just as there is no similarity between '1' and a unit. The diversity of languages makes this point clearly – the same animal can be dog or Hund or 狗. The connection between language and things appears to be arbitrary, but if truth is a property of language, then it seems that truth itself is arbitrary. More exactly, truth is conventional. A proposition is true only because we have all agreed on certain definitions in this particular language. Leibniz's response to this problem relies again on his concept of expression:

> Even though the characters are arbitrary, their use and connection have something that is not arbitrary, namely, a certain correspondence between characters and things, and certain relations among different characters expressing the same things. And this correspondence or this relation is the ground of truth. For it brings about that whether we use these characters or others, the same thing always results, or at least something equivalent, that is, something corresponding in proportion always results. (AG 270)

As we have seen, expression does not require any similarity in the elements of each system, but requires that the two systems of elements maintain the same relations. A proposition then is true when it links words together in the same way that the things the words represent are linked. The word 'fastest' has no necessary connection to the idea of the greatest speed and we could easily choose any other word to represent that idea, just as we could choose any other word to represent motion. Nonetheless, under proper analysis, no matter what two arbitrarily chosen words we use, we will find that they cannot be combined, that the fastest motion is contradictory in any language. Leibniz applies this analysis to the distinction between nominal and real definitions. Nominal definitions, which only let us recognize the concept a word refers to, can be arbitrary and conventional, but real definitions, which establish the possibility of a concept, are not (DM 24; AG 57). This explanation of language based on expression also explains the possibility of translation. A connection of ideas can be translated into other sign systems by maintaining the proper relations between those signs. Thus Leibniz follows the above quotation with the claim that we can perform the same mathematical calculations with different symbols and get the same result, as we can conduct the same calculations with a decimal, duodecimal, or binary system.

For the most part, the sign system in which we reason is that of ordinary language, but the ambiguity and inefficiency of our everyday ways of talking create problems for philosophical reasoning. In fact, Leibniz thinks the large majority of philosophical disputes are driven by the careless use of language, a point also emphasized by many of his contemporaries. Leibniz writes:

> I notice that most people who take pleasure in the science of mathematics have no taste for metaphysical meditations; they find enlightenment in the one, and darkness in the other. The main cause of this seems to be that general notions, which are thought to be the best known, have become ambiguous and obscure because of people's negligence and the inconsistent way in which they explain themselves. And ordinary definitions, far from explaining the nature of things, do not even explain the meaning of words. (WF 140)

This misuse of language explains why proper metaphysics or 'first philosophy' has not yet been found. In using ordinary language we must be careful to give words real definitions and then to use them consistently, but much of Leibniz's effort was directed toward avoiding the problems of ordinary language by developing artificial sign systems. For Leibniz, the strength of a language or sign system lies in its expressive power, not in our usual sense of its ability to express complex feelings but rather in its ability to fully, accurately, and explicitly represent the actual relations between ideas. More specifically, a system of signs must balance the ability to express complex relations between and within ideas with the need for easy and convenient calculation. The role of signs as a replacement for memory also requires that arguments be easily verifiable, so that we can check an argument as we check the strength of a chain – we cannot judge it all at once but if we check every link one by one, we know the whole chain is strong (NE 360). The balance between these different demands can be drawn in different ways, depending on the purpose of the sign system and on which relationships must be most clear. For example, in mathematics, Leibniz developed a binary mathematics, which used two digits instead of ten. He notes that this mathematics is too cumbersome for most calculations, but particularly clear for others. He had no way to know how true the latter claim would turn out to be – computer programming now uses a binary system similar to that developed by Leibniz. Leibniz attributes his invention of calculus not to a moment of mathematical genius, but rather to the invention of a system of signs that allowed certain relationships to be expressed and manipulated. Although Leibniz's main efforts were in logic and mathematics, his concern with signs extends in many directions. In the *New Essays*, he describes a method of bookkeeping he developed through his work in supervising mining operations in the Hartz mountains, a method that would allow an auditor to check the accuracy of all calculations more easily (NE 360). He envisions a written language consisting of pictures, which would be accessible to the illiterate and to people in any culture. This language would be particularly valuable in recapturing some of the vividness that is lost in using blind reasoning: 'this way of writing would be of great service in enriching our imaginations and giving us thoughts that were less blind and less verbal than our present ones are' (NE 398). He seems to think that a little diagram of Hell would motivate us more than the letters H-e-l-l.

Leibniz devised various systems of symbolic reasoning, but his greatest goal was to develop what he called a 'universal character-istic', a kind of perfect logic that would allow us to settle philoso-phical disputes as easily as mathematicians perform calculations. Leibniz's views of both the possibility and form of this character-istic varied over time, but the basic idea is that it would not be a merely formal logic. Beside a system for correctly combining ideas, ensuring that arguments maintain the proper *form*, it would also include an alphabet of human ideas. In an early essay, Leibniz explains,

> When, through my eagerness for this project, I applied myself more intently, I inevitably stumbled onto this wonderful obser-vation, namely, that one can devise a certain alphabet of human thoughts and that, through the combination of the letters of this alphabet and through the analysis of words produced from them, all things can both be discovered and judged. (AG 6–7)

Leibniz's plan seems to be that simple ideas would each have a sign like a letter of the alphabet, so that complex ideas could then be spelled out through the simple ideas composing them. The system would be designed so that we could immediately see if the components of any idea were compatible, thus allowing us easily to know that a concept is truly an idea and to know which ideas can be combined and which cannot. As one might expect, the greatest difficulty was in creating the basic alphabet, and although Leibniz discusses several approaches, including modifying Chinese characters, he made little progress. His dream of this 'universal characteristic', however, remains an interesting illustration both of the importance he attributed to signs and of what a system of signs should ideally accomplish.

IV. IDENTITY AND CHOICE

We have seen that human beings differ from other monads both in the clarity and distinctness of their perceptions and in their ability to grasp necessary truths through innate ideas. The other key difference is in how God treats human beings. In the *Monadology*, after saying that rational minds express the mind of God, Leibniz continues:

> That is what makes minds capable of entering into a kind of society with God, and allows him to be, in relation to them, not only what an inventor is to his machine (as God is in relation to the other creatures) but also what a prince is to his subjects, and even what a father is to his children. From this it is easy to conclude that the collection of all minds must make up the city of God, that is, the most perfect possible state under the most perfect of monarchs. ... This city of God, this truly universal monarchy, is a moral world within the natural world, and the highest and most divine of God's works. (M 84–6; AG 223–4)

The moral quality that makes human beings citizens of this City of God depends on the special status of human identity and of human action, both of which allow us to be held accountable for our actions. The foundation for Leibniz's account of identity lies in the 'complete concept' theory examined in chapter 2. In a letter to Arnauld, Leibniz explains that what made him the same person while he was in Hannover and while he was travelling around Italy is that both events are contained in his complete concept (AG 73). We have seen that what makes something a substance is that its concept contains predicates sufficient to explain its precise relationship to the rest of the universe. Thus the complete concept of a monad gives it a precise identity, sufficient not only to distinguish it from everything else in the world but even to distinguish it from any other possible thing. Leibniz emphasizes this point in his discussion with Arnauld, claiming that God does not have a vague concept of an Adam that could do this or that, but rather a specific concept of this Adam who did exactly these actions, along with an infinite number of concepts of other Adams whose actions are slightly different (WF 99). The creation of those other Adams, of course, would have entailed the creation of a different world. The very completeness of the identity of substances may seem to blur the differences between them – if every created substance contains the entire universe, aren't all of their predicates ultimately the same? As we have seen, variation between monads expressing the same world comes from differences in how much of the world they distinctly perceive and from differences in which parts of the world they perceive more distinctly. In other words, the identity of a monad lies in the particularity of the point of view from which it unfolds the world.

All the predicates of a monad are interconnected, just as everything in the world is related. The present moment of a monad implicates everything else – its past, its future, the whole universe. The true identity of a monad lies in this interconnection of its predicates, in the fact that its identity at one moment cannot be separated from all its other predicates. This emphasis on interconnection appears in a passage responding to Locke. Locke's account of identity is too complex to discuss in detail here, but the relevant issue is the way Locke tries to separate identity based on substance from personal identity. We have seen that substance functioned as a means of individuation, which is to say that substance functioned as a way of identifying things. To say that this is the same *thing* is to say that it is the same *substance*. Locke argues on the contrary that personal identity – that which makes us identify our self or others as the same *person* – is not directly based on remaining the same substance. Rather, personal identity is constructed from memory and experience. Locke suggests a thought experiment which separates substance and memory. What if the soul/substance of person A was stripped of its memories and experiences and given the memories and experience of person B? On the level of substance, the resulting being would still be person A, but Locke argues that we and they would all identify that being as person B. That is, we would identify according to our memories and experience, not according to substance. Leibniz begins by rejecting Locke's experiment –

> An immaterial being or spirit cannot 'be stripped of all' perception of its past existence. It retains impressions of everything which has previously happened to it, and it even has presentiments of everything which will happen to it; but these states of mind are mostly too minute to be distinguishable and for one to be aware of them, although they may perhaps grow some day. It is this continuity and interconnection of perceptions which make someone really the same individual ... (NE 239)

What establishes the identity of a thing is not just its present consciousness or even its conscious memories but the way that awareness is integrated with its past and future and ultimately its existence as one perspective on the universe. On this level, Leibniz's account of identity applies equally to all monads: even a tree has a complete concept in which God would see all of its predicates together. He continues the above passage, though, with an additional kind of identity: '... but our awareness – i.e. when we are aware of past states of mind – prove a moral identity as well, and make the real identity appear' (NE 239). Earlier in his discussion, he makes the same distinction in terms of the real self, which constitutes true identity and contains its full past and future, and the appearance of that self, which adds personal identity (NE 237). Leibniz here uses Locke in his typical way, agreeing with Locke's empirical account while arguing that this experience must be grounded in and inseparable from its connections to everything else.

Personal identity follows from an intersection of apperception, memory, and abstraction (M 30; AG 217). To identify as one person requires that we be aware of our perceptions, that we remember having been aware of other perceptions, and that we then abstract out a self that was the same while having different perceptions. This process is only possible for rational minds that express the mind of God. Abstraction requires that we move from the consideration of particular existing things to the consideration of possibles, to the thought of a self that *could* exist in this or that particular situation but is not reducible to them. Personal identity makes us morally accountable and marks our most significant difference from other animals:

> But the principal difference is that they [animals] do not know what they are nor what they do, and consequently, since they do not reflect on themselves, they cannot discover necessary and universal truths. It is also because they lack reflection about themselves that they have no moral qualities. As a result, though they may pass through a thousand transformations, like those we see when a caterpillar changes into a butterfly, yet from the moral or practical point of view, the result is as if they had perished; indeed, we may even say that they have perished physically, in the sense in which we say that bodies perish through their corruption. But the intelligent soul, knowing what it is – having the ability to utter the word 'I,' a word so full of meaning – does not merely remain and subsist metaphysically, which it does to a greater degree than the others, but also remains the same morally and constitutes the same person. For it is memory or the knowledge of this self that renders it capable of punishment or reward. (DM 34; AG 65–6)

This passage reflects a point Leibniz frequently emphasizes, particularly in his criticisms of Descartes – it is not sufficient to prove that souls are naturally indestructible. Such indestructibility would be meaningless without also preserving personal identity. Leibniz gives an example: imagine that you could suddenly become the King of China, but at the same time you would lose all memory of and connection to your current life (AG 243). Would this be any different from being annihilated at the same time that a new person was created as King of China? That is, while you as monad would continue to exist, you as a *person* would not. Leibniz makes the same point in the above passage when he says that animal souls are all immortal but that from a practical point of view they do perish, because they lose their memories. For Leibniz, future rewards and punishments would neither be fair nor relevant without preservation of memory and personal identity, which is why justice applies only to human beings, not animals or stones, even though their monads are no less eternal.

The actions of a monad cannot be separated from its identity – my identity is the totality of my actions, and my ability to identify myself over time and consciously deliberate are what make my actions morally significant. This connection goes to the very foundation of what it is to be a substance, which is to have internal force and a diverse content:

> It follows from what we have just said that the monad's natural changes come from an *internal principle*, since no external cause can influence it internally (sec. 396, 400). But, besides the principle of change, there must be *diversity in that which changes*, which produces, so to speak, the specification and variety of substances. (M 11–12; AG 214)

This detailed specification is the substance's perceptions, in the broad sense that all monads have perception. Appetition, then, is the force which drives the transition from one perception to another (M 14–15; AG 214–15). These two elements are inseparable. Every thought is an action. Every perception exerts some force for change; even unrecognized perceptions lead to instinctive drives that influence behaviour. At the same time, the actual direction of appetition is determined by the options presented in perception. While all monads have perception and appetition in the broad sense, if a monad's perceptions are utterly confused, its internal force is blindly determined. As perceptions become more distinct, this force becomes something more like what we recognize as desire, and at a higher level of distinctness, it becomes will or volition. Because human beings have distinct perceptions which our will then tends towards, Leibniz says that we can be determined by final causes, that is, by goals. Monads with less distinct perception never know or control where they are going.

The account of human motivation in the early modern period is quite complex. As with many other aspects of early modern thought, it primarily consists in trying to reconcile traditional ideas with accurate accounts of human experience and scientific accounts of the physical world. Throughout this period, two models dominate conceptions of human choice. The first is that human choices come from a will that is radically free, a will that makes choices without being determined by reasons. The second is that human beings choose what they perceive as best. We have already seen that Leibniz follows this latter position, a position with roots in the thought of Socrates and Plato. The problem with both views of choice is that they do not describe desires or emotions very well. Consider falling madly in love with someone. That hardly seems like a choice that follows from a free will – otherwise we could just choose who to fall madly in love with. Life would be a lot simpler. At the same time, my falling in love may not be best; I may even recognize that I would be better off if I did not love this particular person or did not love them quite so madly. Thus in accounting for human choice, the relationship between volition and passion or emotion becomes particularly difficult. These difficulties are entangled in the difficulties of the relationship between mind and body, because mind is associated with will and body is associated with passion. As is generally the case, Leibniz preserves elements of a more traditional account while modifying them to account better for actual experience. We can begin by recalling his definition of will or volition:

> I shall say that volition is the effort or endeavour (conatus) to move towards what one finds good and away from what one finds bad, the endeavour arising immediately out of one's awareness of those things. This definition has as a corollary the famous axiom that from will and power together, action follows; since any endeavour results in action unless it is prevented. (NE 172–3)

To understand this passage, we must keep in mind that volition is just a formation of force. That is, will is not a faculty that chooses where to direct force but rather just is the force or tendency of a mind toward change. In other words, will is not a faculty that chooses what we will desire; it is rather a general term for desire itself, or for a subset of desires. Thus it arises 'immediately out of one's awareness'. The direction of volition follows directly from perception, as the mind immediately and inevitably strives toward whatever it perceives as good. Since volition is striving, action follows directly from it. In God, the will is determined toward what *is* best; in human beings, it is determined toward what *appears* best. The limitations of our perceptions mean that we will sometimes – perhaps often – choose the worst because we see it as the best. This view that human beings necessarily will what

appears best was a common one but it faces an obvious problem –
I know that smoking is bad for me, but I do it anyway. The fact
that we seem to choose to do things that we know are bad is generally called the problem of 'weakness of will'. Leibniz uses
minute and confused perceptions to address the problem. He continues the above passage on volition:

> There are other efforts, arising from insensible perceptions,
> which we are not aware of; I prefer to call these 'appetitions'
> rather than volitions, for one describes as 'voluntary' only
> those actions one can be aware of and can reflect upon when
> they arise from some consideration of good and bad; though
> there are also appetitions of which one can be aware. (NE 173)

Leibniz's most detailed account of appetite is in the *New Essays*.
Locke had argued that human beings always act to reduce a
feeling of *uneasiness*. That is, lacking certain things makes us
uneasy and this feeling of uneasiness forms desire for those things.
This appeal to uneasiness is meant to address weakness of will.
Sometimes something near but not so good makes us more uneasy
than something better but distant. Leibniz praises Locke's
approach but modifies it in a crucial way – the majority of this
uneasiness exists beneath conscious awareness. Leibniz prefers the
French translation of Locke's term – *inquiétude* – which he
connects to a similar German term (*Unruhe*) used to describe the
continually shifting tension that keeps a clock in motion (NE 164–
6). As with the clock, this disquietude keeps our bodies in
constant action. The basis of this disquietude is what Leibniz calls
'semi-sufferings' or 'minute sufferings'. Consider the way we shift
around in a chair without noticing. Something must prompt the
movements of our body, some low level of discomfort we do not
notice. This discomfort can increase until we become noticeably
uncomfortable, if we sit too long or if the chair is particularly
bad. Leibniz's arguments for minute perceptions apply just as well
to minute sufferings. If sitting in the chair did not cause some
vague discomfort, sitting in the chair for a long time would not
cause explicit discomfort. Overall, Leibniz's account of what we
might call minute desires parallels his account of perception, as we
might expect given the inseparability of perception and appetite.
Just as any moment of consciousness involves innumerable minute

perceptions, every moment involves innumerable endeavours toward action. Just as these minute perceptions combine to form the conscious contours of our experience, these minute endeavours combine to form conscious desires and appetites. Finally, just as perceptions can be analysed and better understood, we can deliberate to make conscious choices. Leibniz describes this progression in the *New Essays*:

> For the minute insensible perceptions of some perfection or imperfection, which I have spoken of several times and which are the components of pleasure and pain, constitute inclinations and propensities but not outright passions. So there are insensible inclinations of which we are not aware. There are sensible ones: we are acquainted with their existence and their objects, but have no sense of how they are constituted; these are confused inclinations which we attribute to our bodies although there is always something corresponding to them in the mind. Finally there are distinct inclinations which reason gives us: we have a sense both of their strength and of their constitution. Pleasures of this kind, which occur in the knowledge and production of order and harmony, are the most valuable. (NE 194)

All motivation is determined by perception. In this passage, Leibniz distinguishes three kinds of motivation, based on the clarity of the perceptions that determine it. Some perceptions go entirely unrecognized; these generate habits, instincts, and other actions we do without awareness. Some perceptions are recognized but not clearly understood; these generate appetites and emotions. Finally, some perceptions are recognized and understood; when we act on these perceptions, we can properly be said to choose and to will.

We can begin to examine Leibniz's account of motivation by moving through these three levels. Minute perceptions generate minute pleasures and pains. Leibniz uses these minute pleasures and pains to explain 'choices' we make without conscious thought, for example, whether to step with the right or left foot. Such actions are determined by these unconscious promptings. Although this may seem like a trivial point, it allows Leibniz to maintain that all actions follow from something like appetite and that all actions are determined by a sufficient reason. Seemingly random decisions only seem random. Something prompts our thoughts even in our most relaxed moments and even if this prompting is not something we are aware of. These minute sufferings also explain instinctive reactions. They allow us to react before we would have time to deliberate, yet they do not prompt these reactions through a conscious feeling of suffering or desire. If every breath were prompted by a feeling of explicit pain, we would be miserable most of the time. These instincts also include the ways we naturally think. We have seen how unrecognized innate ideas lead us to organize experience in certain ways.

The next level of motivation is recognized but not fully understood. These desires can be compared to perceptions of colour, which are clear (they can be recognized) but not distinct. Just as colours express combinations of minute perceptions, appetites express combinations of minute desires. These desires function in explaining the conflict between passion and reason. Minute promptings can combine together to overwhelm our decisions to do what we think is best. Thus while the limits of our knowledge explain why we sometimes choose things we think are good but which turn out to be bad, the force of minute perceptions explains why we sometimes choose things that we know are bad. This happens most often when confused perceptions are more vivid than distinct perceptions. For example, a present object of desire can have more force than our distinct knowledge of a bad but distant consequence. Leibniz often blames the 'blindness' of our thoughts of the good:

> We often reason in words, with the object itself virtually absent from our mind. But this sort of knowledge cannot influence us – something livelier is needed if we are to be moved. Yet this is how people usually think about God, virtue, happiness; they speak and reason without explicit ideas – it is not that they cannot have the ideas, for they are there in their minds, but that they do not take the trouble to carry the analysis through. (NE 186)

Here we see the ethical application of the earlier discussion of blind thought, particularly why Leibniz might want to form a pictorial language more vivid than words. Leibniz gives many strategies for avoiding acting against what we know is good. In addition to making our knowledge more vivid, we can cultivate pleasures that align more with reason. To oppose dangerous pleasures, Leibniz suggests we take up simple things like farming or gardening. To avoid idleness, we can collect curiosities, conduct experiments, and engage in useful and pleasurable conversation (NE 187). We can internalize rules to rely on in moments of temptation, with the most basic rule being to delay decisions until we have time coolly to reflect. Finally, we can avoid circumstances in which we tend to be dominated by our passions. Leibniz suggests, for example, that a lover might be cured by a long voyage (NE 187).

The apparent opposition between passion and reasoned choice should not be exaggerated or taken to contradict Leibniz's more basic psychological law that human beings always strive toward what seems best. The key to understanding how this principle applies lies in Leibniz's conception of pleasure as a perception of perfection, that is, order and harmony. Even minute desires are directed toward the pleasure found in harmony and order. This conception of pleasure may seem to conflict with our own experience, but Leibniz illustrates it with music. The pleasure we feel in listening to music is a pleasure in order and harmony, even if we do not explicitly recognize that order. Other pleasures are directed toward a certain harmony and order in the body. The problem then is not that pleasure directly results from what is bad but that we can feel pleasure by confusedly sensing what is good while missing what is bad (NE 186). Smoking certainly brings about some order and harmony in the body, at the very least by easing the not-so-minute suffering that is nicotine withdrawal. When we act toward such pleasures, though, we are not aware of the greater disorder they ultimately cause, because the perceptions that motivate us are not adequate – we cannot see all that they involve. Just as inadequate ideas can contain hidden contradictions, inadequate perceptions can contain hidden pains and disorder. As is often the case, Leibniz's account relies on continuity. All motivation is toward perfection and all bad choices come from misperception. Thus the conflict between passion and deliberate choice is really just a more extreme case of choosing what seems best but really is not. Leibniz's claim that all change must come from forces internal to a monad pushes him to an even more extreme use of confused perceptions. If all changes come from within me, then even something like my spilling my coffee must follow from the *appetite* of my monad. Yet there seems to be no sense in which I *want* to spill my coffee. Pierre Bayle uses this point as one of his main objections to Leibniz's system. He first describes a dog happily eating and then struck by a stick. The eating can easily follow from the dog's own appetite, but how can the pain of the stick? Leibniz responds by distinguishing what is *spontaneous* from what is *voluntary*. All changes emerge spontaneously from a monad, but not all changes are voluntary. He explains:

> We must also distinguish between the spontaneous and the voluntary. The principle of change is in the dog, the disposition of its soul moves imperceptibly towards giving it pain: but this is without its knowing, and without its wanting it. The representation of the present state of the universe in the dog's soul produces in it the representation of the subsequent state of the same universe, just as in the things represented the preceding state actually produces the subsequent state of its world. (WF 200)

Since any monad perceives the entire universe, both the stick and its wielder are expressed in the mind of the dog. When the dog shifts from pleasure to pain, these perceptions that were minute become more distinct. This change follows from the internal force of the dog's own monad, but not in accordance with what the dog wants. Leibniz's position makes more sense if we recall his account of causality. Although monads do not interact, we can still speak of causation between them. One monad can be said to cause changes in another when a particular change is more clearly explained by it, which also means that the event and the reasons for it are more clearly expressed in it. Leibniz connects this to pleasure in the *Discourse on Metaphysics*:

> Therefore whenever a change takes place by which several substances are affected (in fact every change affects all of them), I believe that one may say that the substance which immediately passes to a greater degree of perfection or to a more perfect expression exercises its power and *acts*, and the substance

which passes to a lesser degree shows its weakness and *is acted upon*. I also hold that every action of a substance which has perfection involves some *pleasure*, and every passion some *pain* and vice versa. However, it can happen that a present advantage is destroyed by a greater evil in what follows, whence one can sin in acting, that is, in exercising one's power and finding pleasure. (DM 15; AG 48)

When I act on confused perceptions rather than deliberate choice, my choice cannot be clearly explained even by myself – I just felt depressed so I watched television all day. Leibniz claims that the explanation of such events lies more clearly in the body and the rest of the world than in the mind. In this sense, when we act on such promptings we can be said to be *passive* and these promptings themselves can be called *passions*.

We can now consider the third level of motivation, which is conscious choice or will. The basis of Leibniz's account of the will has already been seen in the discussion of God's will in chapter 2. Leibniz's claim that the will always strives toward what seems best may conflict with some of our intuitions about free will. Facing two alternatives, one clearly better than the other, Leibniz denies that we could freely choose the worse alternative. On a deeper level, any claim that the will was not determined by causes would violate the principle of sufficient reason. Furthermore, God's omniscience requires that God know the future, and thus that the future already be determined. For all of these reasons, Leibniz insists that the will is always determined. Leibniz frequently addresses and criticizes the main alternative, that the will arises from 'indifference' or 'equipoise', that is, without any motivation determining it toward one thing or another. We seem to experience this freedom when the reasons for and against something are exactly balanced. In this situation, it seems that we just freely choose. The standard example of equipoise was that of 'Buridan's ass', named after the medieval philosopher Jean Buridan. In Leibniz's version, a hungry ass stands between two equally appealing meadows and thus is equally inclined to graze in each (T 150). If the inclinations are equally balanced, then the ass will either fail to act and so starve or will just choose one meadow over another freely, without any determining reason. Given that starvation in such a situation seems unlikely, the example was taken to illustrate free, undetermined choice. Leibniz criticizes this argument from a number of directions. Equipoise is fundamentally a situation of ignorance and it would be strange if we were more free when we did not know what was right than when we did know it (AG 151). A free person would be one that never knew what to do so always just chose without reason. More importantly, the role of minute perceptions throws into question our own subjective experience of choosing. The fact that I don't know why I made a choice does not prove I had no motivation determining it, because much of our motivation lies below the level of conscious awareness (T 150). Finally, Leibniz denies the very possibility of equipoise. The infinite complexity, interconnection, and dynamism of the world make it impossible for forces to split exactly between two options. Leibniz explains in a letter to Pierre Coste concerning freedom:

> That is what Mr. Bayle, subtle as he was, did not consider well enough when he held that a case similar to Buridan's ass was possible, and that man placed in circumstances of perfect equilibrium could nevertheless choose. For we must say that the case of a perfect equilibrium is chimerical, and never happens, since the universe is incapable of being divided or split into two equal and similar parts. The universe is not like an ellipse or other such oval, where a straight line drawn through its center can cut it into two congruent parts. The universe has no center, and its parts are infinitely varied; thus the case never arises in which everything is perfectly equal and strikes equally on all sides. And although we are not always capable of perceiving all the small impressions that contribute to determining us, there is always something that determines us between two contradictories, without the case ever being perfectly equal on all sides. (AG 195)

The supposition that the forces of the world could split equally depends on abstraction from the actual complexity of the world. In any case, if forces somehow were perfectly balanced, no choice would be possible. Leibniz goes so far as to claim that if multiple worlds were equally most perfect, God could not choose between them and could not create a world at all. The infinite complexity of things, though, ensures that such a balance cannot arise.

On a broader level, Leibniz's defence of his view of will as determined depends on how he construes the alternative – to deny that our choices are determined is to claim that our choices are random. If there is truly no reason for choosing this way or that, then a choice is determined by chance (T 310). Aside from how that conflicts with the principle of sufficient reason, identifying free will with chance contradicts many of our intuitions about morality. Leibniz concludes his broad criticism of indifference or equipoise with this practical emphasis: 'Finally one does not see wherein the perfection of pure indifference lies: on the contrary, there is nothing more imperfect; it would render knowledge and goodness futile, and would reduce everything to chance, with no rules, and measures that could be taken' (T 425). Knowledge would be futile because the basis of choice would be chance rather than knowledge: no matter how much we knew, we might always randomly choose against it. If choices were not based on what seems best, then measures such as punishment could not work to control behaviour. People would spontaneously choose things that would obviously harm them. Moreover, what would it mean to be good or to cultivate one's ethical character if our character does not determine our choices? Why would a truly random choice be worthy of praise or blame? Leibniz continues:

> I think that one is more worthy of praise when one owes the action to one's good qualities, and the more culpable in proportion as one has been impelled by one's evil qualities. To attempt to assess actions without weighing the qualities whence they spring is to talk at random and to put an imaginary indefinable something in the place of causes. (T 426)

He adds that if choices are not determined by the qualities of a person, then we can never rely on a good person to make consistently good choices or to be trustworthy.

One might object that Leibniz has set up a false dichotomy – by free will we neither mean a will that is determined nor a will that is random. Articulating an alternative, though, is difficult. Our concept of responsibility seems to require that the will somehow be responsible for the will, a position that is obviously circular and incoherent. Leibniz points out that it leads to an infinite regress: 'As for *volition* itself, to say that it is the object of free will is incorrect. We will to act, strictly speaking, and we do not will to will; else we could still say that we will to have the will to will, and that would go on to infinity' (T 151; cf. NE 182). The will simply refers to the volitions we have. These volitions can either be determined by who we are, our character, or they could just come from nowhere, from chance, but there is no way to make sense of volition coming from volition itself. More specifically, it seems that to be responsible for our choices, our choices must be determined by who we are. They can neither be determined by something outside our self nor by chance. This is Leibniz's position – choices follow from and are part of our identity as a particular expression of the universe. Our concern for responsibility, though, might push us further. If my choices are determined by who I am, then to be fully responsible, don't I have to also be responsible for my own identity? To have that responsibility, though, I would have to have freely chosen who I am. That, though, would require a will that preceded my self, a will that chose what sort of self I would be. What could determine that will, though? To be responsible for it, it would have to come from my self, as we have said, but then we fall either into a circle or an infinite regress.

The question of whether or not Leibniz himself believes the human will is 'free' depends on what one means by 'free'. In the *Theodicy*, Leibniz lays out three criteria that a choice must meet in order to be called free:

(1) It must involve deliberation and consciousness of alternatives.
(2) It must be spontaneous, meaning that it must originate from the one who acts.
(3) It must be contingent, that is, not absolutely necessary.

Given these criteria, Leibniz claims that human beings have free will. They are able to deliberate and make conscious decisions. Given that monads do not interact, all of their actions spontaneously originate from themselves. Finally, a monad's existence is contingent, not necessary. Leibniz's treatment of the third criterion is tricky, though, as he uses 'necessary' not in contrast to 'undetermined' but in contrast to 'contingent'. As we have seen, necessary truths are those whose opposites are impossible, deriving from the principle of contradiction. Contingent truths are those whose opposites are possible. They get their truth from the principle of sufficient reason and God's choice to create this particular world. In spite of this distinction, though, the contingent truths of Caesar crossing the Rubicon or Leibniz journeying to Italy are no less determined and certain. In relation to the will, Leibniz frequently says that reasons 'incline without necessitating', but 'incline' is misleading. It cannot mean that we might somehow freely choose against these reasons. In the *New Essays*, he explains more fully:

> But choice, however much the will is determined to make it, should not be called absolutely and in the strict sense necessary: a predominance of good of which one is aware inclines without necessitating, although, all things considered, this inclination is determining and never fails to have its effect. (NE 199)

The movement of the will toward what seems good is certain and determined, but it is not necessary, because other worlds are intrinsically possible. Leibniz takes the contingency of the determination of our choices as sufficient for calling the will free.

Regardless of how one defines free will, Leibniz's account raises problems in relation to justice and responsibility, as some people are determined to sin and be punished for it. Even if we justify punishment in pragmatic terms of preventing further harm, it seems that God treats someone like Judas unfairly in creating him determined to sin and then to suffer in Hell for it. Leibniz addresses this problem partly by claiming that the relevant issue for accountability is the relationship between action and will. That is, whether or not someone should be punished depends only on whether or not their action was free in the above sense, that is, that it was done by them after conscious deliberation. Drawing on his legal background, Leibniz says that judges concern themselves with whether or not a person acted maliciously, not why they are malicious (DM 30; AG 61). Leibniz's determinism maintains this connection between action and will:

> The truth is that the necessity contrary to morality, which must be avoided and which would render punishment unjust, is an

insuperable necessity, which would render all opposition una-
vailing, even though one should wish with all one's heart to
avoid the necessary action, and though one should make all
possible efforts to that end. Now it is plain that this is not
applicable to voluntary actions, since one would not do them if
one did not so desire. Thus their prevision and predetermina-
tion is not absolute, but it presupposes will: if it is certain that
one will do them, it is no less certain that one will will to do
them. These voluntary actions and their results will not happen
whatever one may do and whether one will them or not; but
they will happen because one will do, and because one will will
to do, that which leads to them. (T 381)

For Leibniz, we are accountable for our voluntary actions; how
the will is determined is beside the point. Leibniz uses the connection between will and action to address what he sometimes calls
the 'lazy fallacy', which claims that since the future is already
determined, it will come no matter what actions we take. Thus we
need not strive for anything, and we can rest content in our
laziness. Leibniz replies that while the future is determined, it is
determined through the present. Our success or failure is at least
partly determined by our present effort. That effort, of course, is
itself determined, but since we do not know in which way it is
determined, we should simply make the best effort we can.

Even if accountability depends only on willingness, regardless of
whether or not that willingness is determined, the fact that some
people are determined to will badly seems unfair and seems to
shift some blame to God. To understand Leibniz's response to
this problem, we must consider exactly how the will is determined.
We can take the example Leibniz himself uses as the most extreme
case – Judas. If we assume with Leibniz that Judas deliberately
chose to betray Jesus, then his willingness itself makes him
accountable, even though it was determined. Since the will invari-
able inclines toward what seems best, Judas must have been determined to his choice because he perceived it as the best. He must
have seen the good in what would come from betrayal without
seeing the negative consequences that would also follow. We
could trace the sufficient reason for this perception through all the
particular events in his life, but ultimately the reason would lie
in the particular point of view of his monad or soul. That is, the

sufficient reason for this particular choice would involve the entire story of Judas and his place in this world; it would lead to his complete concept. The sufficient reason would be Judas' own identity – he chose betrayal because that is who he is. As Leibniz puts it in the *Theodicy*: 'I have proved that free will is the proximate cause of the evil of guilt, and consequently of the evil of punishment; although it is true that the original imperfection of creatures, which is already present in the eternal ideas, is the first and most remote cause' (T 302–3). Choice is the immediate cause of guilt, but the ultimate cause is our identity, essence, or complete concept. Sin follows because our essence is finite, which means that we cannot always clearly distinguish what is best from what merely seems best. This connection between identity, will, and action allows Leibniz an interesting and subtle response to accusations against God. Judas might still ask accusingly – why did God make me the kind of person who would choose to betray Jesus? This question, though, misunderstands identity. Leibniz says:

> The reply is easy: otherwise he would not be this man. For God sees from all time that there will be a certain Judas whose notion or idea (which God has) contains this free and future action. Therefore only this question remains, why does such a Judas, the traitor, who is merely possible in God's idea, actually exist? But no reply to this question is to be expected on earth, except that, in general, one must say that, since God found it good that he should exist, despite the sin that God foresaw, it must be that the sin is paid back with interest in the universe, that God will derive greater good from it, and that it will be found that, in sum, the sequence of things in which the existence of that sinner is included is the most perfect among all the possible sequences. (DM 30; AG 61)

We have seen that God's understanding does not contain a vague idea of Judas who could will this or that. God's understanding contains an idea of exactly this Judas, inseparable from this particular world, and ideas of many other monads, some of whom differ only slightly from this Judas. Those other monads would require slightly different (and thus less perfect) worlds. We should recall also that these ideas exist independently of God's will. They follow from the necessity of divine intellect, which includes all possible ideas. Thus, strictly speaking, God does not create the *idea* of Judas. He has the idea of this Judas who would betray Jesus simply because that idea is possible and an infinite intellect thinks all possible thoughts. The role of God's will and responsibility is only in deciding which of these possibilities to create. God's will invariably inclines to the best, so God is determined to create the best possible world, of which this particular Judas is a necessary part. That may seem unfair to Judas, but the only alternative for Judas would be non-existence. The only accusation he could make against God would be – why did you create me at all?

Leibniz's discussion of will, identity, and accountability is complex and subtle, drawing together many strands of his thought – the relation between God's will and intellect, the complete concept theory of truth, minute perceptions, this being the best possible world. It seems to be one of the places where he most struggles to reconcile his account of monads with more traditional views of God, but for this very reason it is perhaps the best display of his philosophical skill. This focus, though, should not distract from the practical implications of his account for such things as regret and responsibility. The logic of regret relies on separating our identity from at least some of our actions. In regret, I assume that I could have made a different choice while still being me. For Leibniz, our identity includes everything we ever do and everything that ever happens to us. All of these have consequences for who we are in the present moment, even though many of those consequences are too minute to be recognized. To regret one aspect of our lives is to wish that our whole identity would change. For Leibniz, to regret is to wish for our own non-existence. It is to wish that I did not exist and that someone slightly different did. In fact, given our own implication in this world, true regret requires wishing both our own non-existence and the non-existence of the world and everything in it. The life-affirming aspect of Leibniz's optimism appears again here. Just as he affirms this flawed world as the best possible, he assumes that we would prefer existence as the flawed people we are over our own non-existence and the existence of someone slightly better.

CHAPTER 5

LEIBNIZ'S PHILOSOPHY AND LEIBNIZ AS PHILOSOPHER

Setting aside questions of his influence and even the correctness of his views, Leibniz is one of the greatest philosophical thinkers in the European tradition. There is a beauty in his ability to interconnect multiple principles, to introduce subtle distinctions, to think issues through to their logical end, to find ways of reconciling conflicting positions. In the dialogues he constructs with other philosophers, he sometimes appears arrogant and even a bit unfair, but at the same time he almost always seems to be the deeper thinker, and, frankly, the better philosopher. This is often true even when his position itself ends up being the wrong one, as in his arguments against Isaac Newton's theory of gravity. Given his skill as a philosopher, there is a certain irony in the fact that he largely ended up on the wrong side of history. Leibniz's influence on the history of philosophy is substantial, but not as deep as his immediate predecessors, René Descartes and John Locke. Many of his metaphysical positions are no longer 'live' options for us, certainly much less so than those of his immediate successors, Immanuel Kant and David Hume. In a way, Leibniz's strength is also one of his weaknesses. He was committed to moderation and reconciliation rather than a revolution in European philosophy. Above all, his greatest goal was to reconcile science, reason, and religion. That path of reconciliation, though, never really succeeded. Now, when science and theology are not seen as antagonists, they tend to exist only in a kind of truce based on a division of labour. Leibniz's vision of good science requiring natural theology and good theology requiring science now seems as naïve and optimistic as his claim that this is the best possible world.

That is not at all to say that Leibniz's philosophical positions are all wrong or outdated, as an exclusive focus on Leibniz's stranger metaphysical claims might suggest. I hope this book has shown how Leibniz's metaphysics generally serves to make coherent his careful and insightful accounts of experience. Many of those accounts remain quite relevant, sometimes almost in spite of his metaphysics. Perhaps the clearest illustration is Leibniz's account of language. On one level, his account fits fully within an early modern view that sees thought as preceding and independent of language, so that language does not shape thought but rather serves it. Such a view is now widely rejected. At the same time, Leibniz's distinction between the ideas innate in us and the concepts or notions that we consciously think fundamentally alters the role of language. Although language does not shape or construct innate ideas, language does shape the actual form of our thinking, playing a constitutive role. That view of language remains quite relevant and was considerably ahead of its time. Similarly, no one would now accept Leibniz's account of the mind as consisting of innate ideas, but his attempt to describe principles which serve as the unrecognized 'muscles and tendons' of thought resembles a number of contemporary theories. His account of minute perceptions and their unrecognized influence on our actions comes quite close to current ideas of the unconscious. More broadly, his attempt to blur the boundaries between consciousness and unconsciousness and animal and human all have contemporary relevance. On most of these issues, Leibniz was far ahead of his time, even if his metaphysics itself was not.

We tend the weigh a philosopher's significance in the history of philosophy by their influence on later philosophers. On this ground, Leibniz is quite significant, most directly for his influence on Kant but also for his influence on twentieth-century philosophy. It is not insignificant that John Dewey and Bertrand Russell both wrote their first books on Leibniz and that Edmund Husserl explicit appeals to Leibniz in describing the ego as a 'monad'.[1] In a way, though, Leibniz's greatest historical significance comes from a different direction. Leibniz's philosophy is one of the most thorough, careful, and coherent attempts to think through the basic assumptions of modern European thought. He represents one culmination of a certain kind of metaphysical thinking, which makes him indispensable for understanding early modern thought and its implications. For example, what are the consequences of the belief that the basic constituents of the world must be independent substances? Leibniz brilliantly shows the contradictions and difficulties that follow from such an assumption, making a good case that if one thinks it through coherently, they must conclude that bodies are not fully real and that substances cannot interact. If one accepts that an all-good and all-powerful God created the world, Leibniz shows well that it must also be the case that this world is the best possible, and he provides perhaps the strongest possible defence of that claim. If one accepts the principle of sufficient reason as absolute, Leibniz shows that this contingent world must be explained by the choice of a being whose existence and nature are necessary. For those who wish to hold on to these kinds of metaphysical assumptions, particularly for those committed to philosophical theology, Leibniz remains one of the most valuable philosophers to read, but even for those who would now reject such assumptions, Leibniz is essential for understanding them and their influence on European thought.

In closing, we should consider not only Leibniz's philosophy, which has been the focus of this book, but also Leibniz as a philosopher. Leibniz stands out for doing well what philosophers still do, that is, for the coherence and complexity of his thinking, but he also stands out for ways in which he contrasts our current conception of what it is to be an academic philosopher. Leibniz was profoundly committed to the idea of bringing together different points of view. He writes of philosophy in his own time –

> So I wish that men of intellect would seek to gratify their ambition by building up and moving forward, rather than by retreating and destroying. I would rather they emulated the Romans who built fine public works than the Vandal king whose mother advised him that since he could not hope for renown by rivalling those magnificent structures he should seek to destroy them. (NE 100–1)

Leibniz urged his contemporaries to build on and use what was strong in other theories rather than criticizing what was weak. While Leibniz was not always as open-minded and conciliatory as his ideals suggest, his belief that every point of view expresses the truth in a different way did lead to a concern with exchange and mutual understanding, and this had political implications, particularly in his hope to use philosophy as a foundation for religious reconciliation, a problem as relevant in our time as it was in that of Leibniz. Leibniz was almost alone among his contemporaries in applying such an approach to cultures outside of Europe as well, or at least to China. In a time when philosophers seem set on resisting globalization as long as possible, we might still have something to learn from Leibniz's concern with diversity, exchange, and mutual understanding.

On a broader level, Leibniz was a paradigmatic 'public intellectual', focused at least as much on political activities as on his own research. He was fully committed to a reciprocal relationship between society and intellectuals. He writes in a letter to Czar Peter the Great:

> Although I count many years of service in administration and law, and though I have been consulted for a long time by great princes, I nevertheless consider the arts and sciences as more elevated, and capable of increasing the glory of God and the welfare of mankind, for it is especially in the sciences and knowledge of nature and art that we see the wonders of God. ... I should regard myself very proud, very pleased and highly rewarded to be able to render Your Majesty any service in a work so worthy and pleasing to God; for I am not one of those impassioned patriots of one country alone, but I work for the well-being of the whole of mankind, for I consider heaven as my country and cultivated men as my compatriots...[2]

On one side, intellectuals have a responsibility to promote the public good, through education and policy debate but also through the concrete application of knowledge. Leibniz particularly emphasized the importance of improving the practice of medicine. Leibniz himself participated in many of the social issues of the day, from encouraging a more accommodating approach to Chinese culture, to promoting harmony and reconciliation between different Christian factions, to opposing French expansionism. At the same time, Leibniz realized that the development of knowledge depended more on social institutions than on individual effort and genius. He worked tirelessly to promote public support for research and to create institutions for the exchange and promotion of knowledge. Leibniz's confidence in the alignment of the progress of knowledge and promotion of the common good supports the image of him as a bit naïve and optimistic, but in a time so cynical about the public role of intellectuals, a bit of Leibnizian optimism may not be a bad thing.

REFERENCES

CHAPTER I

1 See Voltaire, *Candide, or Optimism*, trans. J. Butt (New York: Penguin Classics, 1950). Dr Pangloss, Candide's tutor, is generally taken as a satire of Leibniz, although the satire is probably more directly aimed at popular and less sophisticated versions of Leibniz's position, such as that of Alexander Pope.
2 Biographical details in the sections are taken from J. Aiton, *Leibniz: A Biography* (Boston: Adam Hilger Ltd, 1985).
3 For a brief example of these kinds of negotiations, see the excepts from two letters to Jacques-Benigne Bossuet in *Leibniz: Political Writings*, ed. and trans. Patrick Riley (Cambridge: Cambridge University Press, 1992), pp. 188–91.
4 René Descartes, *The Philosophical Writings of Descartes*, ed. and trans. J. Cottingham, R. Stoothoff, D. Murdoch, and A. Kenny (Cambridge: Cambridge University Press, 1994), v. II, p. 16.
5 Leibniz deals with the sacraments or 'Mysteries' in many places, particularly in the *Theodicy*, but the clearest example of his tendency to accommodate himself to the perspectives of his correspondents is his exchange with the Jesuit Bartholomaeus Des Bosses, in which Leibniz develops the idea of a 'substantial chain' in an attempt to reconcile his account of bodies with the transubstantiation of bread into the body of Christ. This 'substantial chain' appears nowhere else in Leibniz's writings. For excerpts from the Des Bosses correspondence, see AG 197–206.
6 G. W. Leibniz, *Philosophical Papers and Letters*, ed. and trans. Leroy Loemker (Dordrecht: D. Reidel, 1969), p. 207.

CHAPTER 2

1 For Spinoza's position, see *Ethics*, Part I, Proposition 16 and its corollaries, Proposition 17 scholium 1, and Proposition 33 and its scholia.

2 Spinoza, *Ethics*. Part 1, Proposition 33, scholium 2, in *The Collected Works of Spinoza*, Volume I., ed. and trans. Edwin Curley (Princeton: Princeton University Press, 1985).

3 The difficulty of these issues is reflected by their persistence in the tradition of Western philosophy. The issue Leibniz deals with here is essentially the question raised by Socrates in the *Euthyphro*: is the pious pious because the gods love it, or do the gods love it because it is pious?

4 *Leibniz: Political Writings*, p. 83.

5 *Leibniz: Political Writings*, p. 47.

6 Descartes recognizes this problem and thus believes the only way necessary truths can be relied on is if we prove that God is good and will not deceive us. Leibniz's analysis, though, points out a fundamental problem in Descartes' argument – if the nature of goodness (i.e., that it excludes deception) is arbitrarily chosen by God, we cannot assume God will not at some time change the meaning of goodness so as to include deception.

7 Descartes, *The Philosophical Writings of Descartes*, v. 11, p. 37.

8 Hume, *Dialogues Concerning Natural Religion* (New York: Prometheus Books, 1989), p. 93. This discussion takes place in Part II of 'Dialogues Concerning Natural Religion'.

9 This position is central in Descartes' account of error. In the fourth meditation, he writes:

> I realize that I am, as it were, something intermediate between God and nothingness, or between supreme being and non-being: my nature is such that in so far as I was created by the supreme being, there is nothing in me to enable me to go wrong or lead me astray; but in so far as I participate in nothingness or non-being, that is, in so far as I am not myself the supreme being and am lacking in countless respects, it is no wonder that I make mistakes. I understand, then, that error as such is not something real which depends on God, but merely a defect. (Descartes, *The Philosophical Writings of Descartes*, v. II, p. 38)

10 See Hume, *Dialogues Concerning Natural Religion*, particularly Part II.

CHAPTER 3

1 For Locke's discussion of substance, see John Locke, *An Essay Concerning Human Understanding*, ed. P. Nidditch (Oxford: Clarendon Press, 1975), Book II, chapter XXIII, pp. 295–317.

2 Zeno's paradoxes use this point to argue that motion is impossible. Leibniz briefly addresses this and sees it as resulting from the confusion of the ideal and the real. That is, the impossibility of motion only follows from erroneously taking space, time, and motion, which involve continua, as real rather than ideal. See WF 207.

3 Spinoza claims that all things are animate in *Ethics*, Part II, Proposition 13, scholium.

4 For Bayle's argument, see the excerpts in WF 194–7 and 224–32.

5 For Malebranche's discussion of the relationship between mind and body, see Nicolas Malebranche, *Dialogues on Metaphysics and Religion*, ed. and trans. N. Jolley and D. Scott (Cambridge: Cambridge University Press, 1997), dialogue seven.

CHAPTER 4

1 Locke, *An Essay Concerning Human Understanding*, Book I, ch. 2, p. 50.

2 This position runs throughout *An Essay Concerning Human Understanding*, but is most directly discussed in Book II, chs. 1, 2, 12.

3 For Malebranche's view of vision in God, see *Dialogues on Metaphysics and Religion*, first and second dialogues; and *The Search After Truth*, Book Three, Part Two, chapters 1–7; Book Five, chapter 5; and Elucidation X. He distinguishes his own position from that of Augustine in Book Three, Part Two, chapter 6 of *The Search After Truth*.

4 See Locke, *An Essay Concerning Human Un*derstanding, Book II, chapter 1.

5 Descartes, v. II, p. 24.

6 For Hobbes' view of language and truth, see Thomas Hobbes, *Leviathan*, Part I, chapter 4, where he says '... truth consisteth in the right ordering of names in our affirmations ...' *Leviathan*, ed. R. Tuck (Cambridge: Cambridge University Press, 1996), p. 28.

CHAPTER 5

1 John Dewey's *Leibniz's New Essays Concerning the Human Understanding* (New York: Hillary House, 1961) appeared in 1886. Bertrand Russell's *A Critical Exposition of the Philosophy of Leibniz* (London: Routledge, 1992) first appeared in 1900. Edmund Husserl explicitly appeals to Leibniz in the *Cartesian Meditations* (Boston: Kluwer, 1993), published in 1931.

2 P. Wiener, trans., *Leibniz Selections* (New York: Charles Scribner's Sons, 1951), pp. 596–7.

BIBLIOGRAPHY

Aiton, E. J. *Leibniz: A Biography*. Boston: Adam Hilger Ltd, 1985.

Descartes, René. *The Philosophical Writings of Descartes*. Cottingham, J., Stoothoff, R., Murdoch, D., and Kenny, A. (eds and trans.). 3 vols. Cambridge: Cambridge University Press, 1994.

Dewey, John. *Leibniz's New Essays Concerning the Human Understanding*. New York: Hillary House, 1961.

Hobbes, Thomas. *Leviathan*. Tuck, R. (ed.). Cambridge: Cambridge University Press, 1996.

Hume, David. *Dialogues Concerning Natural Religion*. New York: Prometheus Books, 1989.

Husserl, Edmund. *Cartesian Meditations*. Cairns, D. (trans.). Boston: Kluwer, 1993.

Leibniz, G. W. *Leibniz Selections*. Wiener, P. (ed. and trans.). New York: Charles Scribner's Sons, 1951.

Leibniz, G. W. *Philosophical Papers and Letters*. Loemker, L. (ed. and trans.). Dordrecht: D. Reidel, 1969.

Leibniz, G. W. *Leibniz: Political Writings*. Riley, P. (ed. and trans.). Cambridge: Cambridge University Press, 1992.

Locke, John. *An Essay Concerning Human Understanding*. Nidditch, P. (ed.). Oxford: Clarendon Press, 1975.

Malebranche, Nicolas. *Dialogues on Metaphysics and Religion*. Jolley, N. and Scott, D. (eds and trans.). Cambridge: Cambridge University Press, 1997.

Malebranche, Nicolas. *The Search After Truth*. Lennon, T. M. and Olscamp, P. J. (eds and trans.). Cambridge: Cambridge University Press, 1997.

Russell, Bertrand. *A Critical Exposition of the Philosophy of Leibniz*. London: Routledge, 1992.

Spinoza, Benedict. *The Collected Works of Spinoza, Volume I*. Curley, E. (ed. and trans.). Princeton: Princeton University Press, 1985.

Voltaire. *Candide, or Optimism*. Butt, J. (trans.). New York: Penguin Classics, 1950.

INDEX